Radical Reframe

Change the Stories that Shape Your Life

Lara Kain PA-C, MPAS

ISBN: 1542912563
ISBN 13: 9781542912563

This book is dedicated to my first earth school teachers: my biological father, James Calvin Bristow and my grandfather, George Henry Phillips. Thank you for paving the way to the birthing of this book.

The Dragonfly

Ancient, wise, dragonfly spirit
Master of transformation and evolution
Teach me to dance upon the winds of change
To maintain my inner light even in the worst of times
And trust my own evolution

Show me the beauty of my life
Help me to see beyond the illusion of my ego
To see each day as a precious gift
And know each person has a sacred purpose to reveal

Teach me grace through transformation
To always turn my heart towards the light
For the light will burn away all that is not true
Leaving only love in its wake

Help me to embrace growth and pain and suffering
As the pathway to beauty and grace and wisdom
Guide me through this dream of life
Keep my spirit steady and strong in the knowledge that
I have value
That my life transcends the mists of my illusions

*A*cross the globe, the dragonfly symbolizes renewal and trans-formation. They represent the realm of the mystical and offer an invitation to consider the deeper meaning of life. Having inhabited our planet for almost 300 million years, they are masters of adaptation and change.

Table Of Contents

The Dragonfly   v

Introduction: The Disempowerment of the Modern Human Being   ix

1   The Radical Reframe Solution: You've got The Power!   1

2   Awareness: Waking up from the Dream   19

3   Emotions: Your Personal Navigational System   38

4   Triggers: The Gift Within the Rub   60

5   What's Your Story, Morning Glory?   77

6   Boundaries: Where You End and Others Begin   98

7   The Reframe:The Art of Self Empowerment   115

8   Going Deeper Within: Cultivating Self Compassion   134

Epilogue   153

Acknowledgements   157

Introduction: The Disempowerment of the Modern Human Being

"Most people walk through the world in a trance of disempowerment. Our work is to transform that into a trance of empowerment."

Dr. Milton H. Erickson

"If you change the way you look at things, the things you look at change."

Wayne Dyer

The Reframe that Changed My Life

I have come to see my life as a progression of reframes. Looking back I understand there were times when I was in so much pain, or so off course from my true calling, that I was forced to reconsider my path altogether and make a dramatic right, or left turn. These times were certainly the most difficult and yet also the most rewarding. They are the defining moments of our lives: they build character, resolve and cultivate a true self knowing. The most significant reframe of my life thus far came when I was 37. It was the first time I actively applied the Radical Reframe principals I am going to teach you in this book: Stop, Center, Inquire and Reframe. Don't worry if you have no idea what I am talking about, after you finish this book you will be a master of the Radical Reframe process.

I had been working with a meditation teacher for about 4 years and had been married for 2. My meditative practice helped me to see how I was prone to distort the truth when reality showed me something that was painful or I did not like. My tendency would be to create a story about what was happening around me to skirt responsibility for that which I did not want to acknowledge or take responsibility for in my life. My teacher would often say, "an emotion expressed is an emotion repressed." Being a bit of a drama queen, I initially balked at this ridiculous notion of emotions, and yet, as I cultivated a relationship with my inner self, I began to understand how the expression of strong emotions was really *a habituated reaction to a belief, and not an authentic experience of a feeling.*

With this awareness I started to more closely observe myself, and my emotional reactions, in particular, how I reacted to anger. I realized my reactions were polarized depending on whether or not there was alcohol involved. A pattern emerged: if all parties were sober, when I felt a strong negative emotional reaction I tended to respond by freezing, like a frightened rabbit. I would shut off my feelings and stuff them deep inside. If alcohol was involved, my reaction was to push back with anger. Considering that some of the most frightening moments of my childhood involved an intoxicated adult, I began to see why I had such differing reactions. This became a very obvious pattern in my romantic relationships, as I had a habit of dating people who had an unhealthy relationship with alcohol and had married a man who was an alcoholic.

This particular incident occurred one night while I was getting ready for bed. I was standing in my bathroom holding a brush in my hand and watching myself turn to face my husband as he entered. His face was red, and he was yelling about something I had done. I immediately recognized he had been drinking and I thought to myself, watch yourself Lara, this is a trigger for you because you feel afraid that he seems out of control. I consciously stopped my train of thought and the cascade of assumptions I was making about not feeling safe and being victimized. Instead, I started to focus on my breathing and observed what was happening with as much curiosity as I could conjure. For the first time in my life I realized I had a choice. I did not have to revert to my habituated behavior of lashing out with anger when someone was drinking and felt out of control to me. I could just observe the interaction as it was unfolding and know that I was in control and capable of taking care of myself and my safety.

This switch was possible because I had practiced being aware of my feelings and was able to acknowledge them: I was scared. In that moment I realized I did not have to play the victim role from a past story - believing I was inherently in danger because someone with whom I was interacting was intoxicated. Instead, in that beautiful moment, I was free to choose how I was going to react. I was *free*. So instead of reverting to anger, I chose to reframe this situation. I calmly looked at my husband and said, "We have a choice. I am no longer going to engage in this dance with you, so you can leave, and go calm down, or I will leave, but I will no longer endure the brunt of your anger."

The reaction was astounding. The abrupt pattern interrupt stopped him in his tracks. He was so used to my fighting back, he did not know how to respond. So he turned around, got his keys and left. That was the day the yelling ended in my house. It ended because I had cultivated an ability to witness my emotions and myself and consequently learned to make better choices about how to handle difficult situations. Choices not based on my past wounds, but based on who I wanted to be *now*, and how I wanted to live my life. At that point I wanted to live a life with less drama. I will tell you, after my husband left, I felt my body start to shake as my brain was pumping out high doses of fear hormones into my blood stream. I had reframed how I was responding to the situation: it would take months for my brain chemistry to rewire itself, therefore I still had the same physiological reaction. But the awareness was different. I had the space within myself to realize I no longer wanted to be that angry, victimized person. In that one moment, I had the power to choose a different story. And I chose one where I was in control, and reframed the entire situation so that it ended with me feeling empowered. It radically changed my life.

As I See It

I believe we are extraordinarily sensitive organisms that have a pivotal place within this rich tapestry of life on earth. In our evolution, though, we have learned how to manipulate our environment to maximize our feelings of security and safety, shifting our place in nature from that of *prey to predator to dominator*. We have pulled ourselves out of the natural ecosystem and surrounded ourselves instead with brick and mortar. Soft paths turned to cement sidewalks, fresh air turned to smog, fresh produce and farm raised foods turned to food products loaded with artificial chemicals and colorings. Instead of eating what we grow, our food is shipped to us from around the world, leaving us with no connection to where the substances that sustain our existence come from. In his TED talk *Teach Every Child About Food*, chef, Jamie Oliver painfully shows the state of our ignorance surrounding food by taking vegetables into a kindergarten class and asking the children to identify them. The children were unable to identify a tomato, potato or onion, effectively demonstrating our culture's complete disconnect from the circle of life. We have lost touch with the truth of who we are as human beings.

Technology has further distanced us from our organic roots by becoming the interface through which we experience our relationships and view our lives. This disconnect makes many of us feel alienated, tired and overwhelmed. Rather than acknowledging our place in the order of things and knowing because we exist we are okay, we look outside of ourselves for assurances that we are good and worthy. What we do, own, or have has come to define us as opposed to who we are as human beings. Our existence has shifted from working to survive within the laws of nature, each day devoted to survival and learning to coexist within the natural world to working in a building, sometimes hundreds of feet above the ground, bathed in artificial light, surrounded by unnatural sounds and eating something that comes out of a machine or package: putting aside our happiness today for the promise of success tomorrow. This disconnect has created a vacuum in our psyches that has become filled with a myriad of stories rationalizing our plight. In essence we have become disempowered beings, believing our moods and our lives in general are at the mercy of our external environments.

In these disconnected states we are perpetually fantasizing about freedom from the chains that bind us. I hear frequently from clients, "I just want to run away," or "if I could just have a week by myself," or the worst of all, "I think about not existing almost everyday." The question is, *what are we really wanting to run away from?* Bad bosses, marriages, family commitments, long hours, low pay, bills? The physical, external things we believe are controlling us or could it be, what we really need to break from is the way we are perceiving our lives?

We have become lost within the virtual world of time and technology and never ending to-do lists. Our culture perpetuates a driving sense of perfection when in reality we are perfectly imperfect. Inner peace comes from a willingness to know and accept our own strengths and imperfections as well as those of others. Through our ability to be open and vulnerable, be comfortable in our human-ness, we experience a sense of connectedness in life and self satisfaction. With this acceptance of what is comes a profound sense of empowerment, as we realize everything is as it should be. The more we fight against reality, the more unhappiness and discontent we feel. What I see repeatedly is people stumbling through their lives feeling less than, alienated, not worthy, not lovable, with an incessant, almost psychotic desire to be perfect. This story of perfection and achieving something outside of ourselves to feel worthy is what is making most of us so miserable.

I believe our lives can be very different from the version most of use are living. When I probe clients about self-care, I hear the following statements: "I don't have time"; "I feel so overwhelmed and tired"; "I feel empty inside"; and the most despairing is "what is the point?" These statements reflect a type of black or white thinking: my life is good, or my life is bad. By making these broad generalizations we rob ourselves of the minute-to-minute beauty of our lives and our experiences as human beings. Pain offers an opportunity for growth and loss cultivates emotional resilience. In our culture, though, we have learned to run from what is perceived as negative emotions and, instead, perpetually chase after happiness.

In the process of forever searching for the big hit, or the magic pill, we have surrendered our personal power to the belief that life should be happy, and if it isn't, there is clearly something wrong. This story of perfection and happiness creates a tendency to ignore that life is a process - a messy, complicated, and at times, painful process. We have missed the point: the gift is in the journey. When we are able to take a step back and see all of the multiple threads that make up our lives, we begin to see the beauty in each one, the good and the bad, the joy and the pain. When we accept life on life's terms, and start to sift through the fiction of our lives and see the facts, we can begin to get honest with who we are and who we want to be.

This is where the artistic venture of life begins: when we begin to understand that we are the creators of our experience through the stories we tell. The rub in life is necessary to get our attention, help us to focus on where we are going and what we are creating, by offering an opportunity to change course at every turn. We can look at our current situations with curiosity and search for ways to grow out of what is no longer needed so we may create something new. This is the foundational principle of the Radical Reframe process: that at any moment you can change the story you are telling and in essence change your life.

We can turn our self-limiting thoughts around to become self-fulfilling achievements. The meaning we ascribe to our lives is the culmination of the stories we have been perpetually, and often unconsciously, telling ourselves, reiterating in multiple versions. These stories translate into our experience. If you are chronically feeling depressed, you will see all the reasons for your depression in your life. If you are intentionally cultivating an attitude of gratitude, you will see more and more reasons to be grateful. As Wayne Dyer puts it, "Loving people live in a loving world. Hostile people live in a hostile world. Same world."

The Radical Reframe process has four principles: Stop, Breathe, Inquire and Reframe. The first step is a process of *self-awareness*, learning to become aware of our emotional state so when we begin to feel off center we know we need to *stop*, and take inventory of what is going on inside and outside of ourselves. The second step is cultivating awareness of our bodies through *breath mindfulness* so we can *center* ourselves and *relax* rather than react. We need to give ourselves space to sift through the facts and fiction, so we may begin to see beyond our limiting stories. The third step is to start *inquiring* about the story we are telling about a given situation. It is the process of *getting curious* about how we are seeing things and expanding our vision into how we might see them differently so we may grow and change. And lastly, *reframing* your interpretation of what is going on both within and without, to be in concert with how you want to feel and where you want your life to go, in this way you may feel *empowered* in every situation of your life.

This process takes a lot of courage and compassion. It can be frightening. When we take responsibility for how we feel and what we have created in our lives, we then become accountable to ourselves and others. This is hard, especially if we have spent a lifetime feeling we need to be perfect in order to be loved, all the while blaming other people and situations for when we feel badly. In the end, the source of our pain originates from within. One of the greatest lies we have been conditioned to believe is that our lives are a consequence of things outside of our control. This process is about taking responsibility for what we have created and redirecting the course of our lives through reframing a new story, one in which we are the creative directors of who we want to be and the type of life we wish to live.

Let's say someone in your life has greatly disappointed and/or hurt you and you hold a lot of resentment towards them. The resentment and anger that you hold towards them is only hurting you for they are continuing to go about their lives. You are essentially giving them the power to hurt you further by holding onto a story of resentment and anger. To free yourself from the grip of anger, you can reframe the story into one of gratitude, being thankful for the opportunity to practice forgiveness or patience, or for the reminder not to take things so seriously.

Our greatest teachers are those that elicit the strongest emotional reactions from us, because when this happens we are able to consciously and objectively consider our pain, we are gifted with the opportunity to heal. These negative stories, ones of anger, victimization, injustice, and shame are the places where reality bumps up against an unresolved wound within ourselves. By taking responsibility for our feelings, and discovering where they might be pointing to something within us that is unresolved, we choose to empower ourselves through accountability and self acceptance.

You can change your perception of anything! Just look at Malala Yousafzai. This amazing Pakistani teen was catapulted into international fame at the age of 14 when she was shot in the head while riding the bus home from school. She was targeted by the Taliban for her human rights advocacy work for women's rights and education in her native Swat Valley, in the Khyber Pakhtunkhwa, northwest Pakistan. Since the assassination attempt, Malala's advocacy has grown into an international movement. At 17, she became the youngest person ever to receive the Nobel Peace Prize. As a young girl she was thrown a major life challenge, and instead of collapsing into a story of victimization and repression, she rose to the challenge, reframed her situation, and became a global inspiration of peace and forgiveness.

We always have a choice! Be miserable or proactive, victimized or empowered, lazy or motivated, you choose where you want your thoughts to be, because remember, *a reframe is just a thought away*. Through this process of reframing, we can become inspiring, loving and uplifting individuals. As Ghandi wisely said, "Be the change you wish to see in the world." Because when you shift your thoughts, the world shifts around you.

～ ～

This books springs out of a disturbing trend I have observed among my patients that I believe transcends all health care. We, as a culture, have become so overwhelmed by our lives that when something goes wrong that we cannot immediately "fix" we feel we have to find the solution "out there." We walk into a doctor's office, hands raised, saying, "fix me." We absolve ourselves of any responsibility for what is occurring in our lives and claiming we do not have the time nor energy to change. Whether it is high blood pressure, migraine headaches or depression, whatever the ailment, we have been conditioned to believe the solution is outside of ourselves. If I had a nickel for every time a client told me they just want a "happy pill," I would be rich! I have found that when people finally make their way to me, sitting in my office prepared to receive a pill that will end their suffering, they feel completely disempowered in their lives. I hear statements such as, "I'm so embarrassed to be here" or "I can't believe I couldn't figure this out on my own", or, "I feel broken" or my favorite, "why can't I be normal?" To which I often retort, "what would normal look like to you?"

We have become enamored with this notion of *normal*, and are constantly chasing this idealized version of what it means to be human, to no avail. We have turned over control of so many aspects of our lives that we feel out of control and disempowered. We spend inordinate amounts of energy trying to achieve what's next: graduation, marriage, a career, buying a house, paying a mortgage, starting a family, retirement. We have lost touch with the natural ebb and flow of life. Everything is measured by society's terms, the great collective story of success, and not *our own* terms. We have lost the wonder of being an individual and this disconnection is causing a great deal of suffering. These timelines are driving us to drink, literally, as we doggedly push to achieve things "on time". And when we don't succeed, we get anxious and depressed making up stories about how "abnormal" we are.

From the time we are born, we receive messages from our caretakers about who we are and the world around us. As our brain grows, we internalize these messages and they become the foundation of our life experience. Unfortunately we are not taught to discern which stories are empowering and which ones are disempowering. These messages are just stories we inherited from the ones who raised us, who learned them from the ones who raised them. They are stories that cloud our ability to see what is real and what is not in this world. Messages that convinced us we have little power over our lives to control or change things, and as a consequence, our potential has become severely limited by our own self-limiting beliefs.

We are perpetually running to catch up: keep up with life, friends and neighbors, and are completely missing what is right in front of us: a soul expanding, mind-blowing human experience filled with a full spectrum of emotional experiences. So I ask you, how many glorious opportunities to live out your dreams are you missing in your life because you are locked into one way of seeing the path?

I'd like to take a moment here to do a little exercise to get a sneak peak at the stories you have in your head. Take a moment and consider what your thoughts focus on throughout the course of your day. Are they anchored in your visions, goals and dreams? Are you constantly reviewing the things and people you love or are excited to meet in the future? Or are you perpetually reenacting your fears and insecurities? Are your thoughts of empowerment and self-love, or do they carry feelings of lack and frustration? If you could pick one or two words to described your most prominent thought-form through out the day, what would it be? And, does this surprise you? Does it support the story of the life you want to lead or does it trap you into a very restricted way of seeing the world?

Your thoughts are constantly creating your reality and only you have the power to change them. By learning to reframe your life narratives you will transform the patterns of your own life as well as the patterns that shape your relationships, communities, and the larger social worlds in which you interact. Norman Vincent Peale, the progenitor of the positive thinking movement, said it perfectly: "change your thoughts and you change your world."

Why Should You Trust Me?
First and foremost, I have walked the walk. I know what it is like to be depressed, anxious, suicidal, and trapped within the confines of an addiction. I have experienced sexual and emotional abuse. I have felt trapped in a job I hated, a marriage that was abusive and I have found myself repeatedly in financial ruin. Looking back, I can honestly say I am one stubborn human being for not seeing the gift in each of these painful life experiences. I believe this book will expedite awareness of your own path to healing and perhaps help you avoid some of the grief and pain I experienced.

Each of those experiences were life's attempt to get my attention, to let me know I was off course, and was trying to give me a opportunity to reconsider my path. Each obstacle was an chance for me to start looking at what I was creating through my self-defeating stories and beliefs. Most of the time I just pushed through, clung to my anger, my feelings of being victimized, and my ever increasing feelings of learned helplessness in life. I allowed the feelings to fester, and for many years directed that anger back at myself in the form of an eating disorder and self sabotaging behaviors.

I believe my first insight of the ability we have to reframe our lives began at age 25 but is still continuing today; I understand now that there is no finish line. This thing called life is a process. It is beautiful, difficult, crazy and painful. It is a perpetual evolution of refining what we focus on. And what we are focusing on is constantly being reflected back to us in the circumstances of our lives. Think of it like this: your life is like a movie, the projector is your mind, the film reel is your thoughts, and what you see on the screen is a consequence of the interaction between the two. When you think positive thoughts you see positive interactions on the screen, and when you think negative thoughts you see negative interactions on the screen. It is as simple as that. If you are seeing lots of pain and discomfort in your life, your thoughts are mainly being focused on pain and discomfort. If you are seeing lots of love and joy in your life, your thoughts are mainly being focused on love and joy.

Secondly, over the past 15 years I have had the honor of witnessing people work through their pain. I am a medically-trained board certified Physician Assistant practicing integrative psychiatry, incorporating my training as a Breath Meditation Facilitator and Holistic Health Coach, to offer clients support balancing their brain chemistry and their lives through pharmaceuticals, supplements, diet, exercise and life coaching. I have had the gift of having people come to me for help in figuring out their lives. I have witnessed great pain, heard horrific stories, observed amazing strength and grace, and have been an integral part of people's healing process. For this opportunity I am deeply grateful.

I have spent hours with clients, coaching them on how to get in touch with their authentic selves. I teach clients meditation and Breathwork, helping them to sift through their own self-defeating stories while sharing a few of my own, enabling them to see their gifts and desires and then turning all this information into a plan of action to rework their life. I feel the excitement over an awareness realized, and can sense the empowerment that comes from clients actively working the Radical Reframe process to completely change the way they are seeing their lives. My clients' successes at getting new jobs, healing relationships and simply feeling happier with their lives is an amazing reward for me, and is what is the driving force behind this book. I feel so inspired by the results I have seen in myself and my clients, I feel driven to get the message out to as many people as I can.

What is this impassioned message, you ask? It is this: how we see our lives is all in our heads, and at the end of the day, we are the ones responsible for how we feel. As Charles Swindoll, the evangelical Christian pastor, so eloquently states: "The longer I live, the more I realize the impact of attitude on life. It is more important than the past, than education, than money, than circumstances, than failure, than successes, than what other people think or say or do. It is more important than appearance, giftedness, or skill. It will make or break a company...a church...a home. The remarkable thing is we have a choice everyday regarding the attitude we will embrace for that day. We cannot change our past...we cannot change the fact that people will act a certain way. We cannot change the inevitable. The only thing we can do is to plan on the one thing we have and that is our attitude. I am convinced that life is 10% what happens to me and 90% of how I react to it."

In my own life and in my client work, I have found the only thing getting in the way of what we want is our story. I am not talking about using positive affirmations, wishing on a star and POOF your life appears before you just as you ordered. Life is messy and most of us don't even know what we feel passionate about much less what we could be doing differently. We begin by getting honest about the current state of our lives and then learn to reframe our stories based on how we want to feel. I promise, just a few tweaks in perspective and you will begin to see how easy it is to embrace life on your life's terms while maintaining a sense of balance and contentedness.

Lastly, I have been on my own spiritual campaign for over 20 years searching for peace within. I have spent years observing my own behaviors, getting honest with myself and those around me, and learning to challenge my self-limiting beliefs and judgments to use them as indicators for how aligned or misaligned I am with my higher self/soul/spirit. In doing this, I have started living a more authentic life. A simpler life, if you will, where I have shed feeling victimized and abused, and moved into a place of feeling empowered. I now live a life with less drama, and more love. I feel secure in my life because I know I can handle anything that is thrown my way, and if I don't have the answers, someone else will. I have come to appreciate that my life is perfectly imperfect and see that everything in it offers an opportunity to release judgement, invite in compassion, and be grateful for the growth opportunities.

I have learned to be more humble. I have learned to expect less and explore more, to be more compassionate with myself and others, to be mindful of the stories I tell and to trust that people love me and care for me even when I make mistakes. I have learned to look outside of my programmed expectations for possible answers, and to talk it out and trust I will be heard and that there is a solution to every problem. And lastly, I have learned it is okay to walk away when I do not believe something is in my highest good. This process works: each time I am able to catch myself telling a disempowering story about my life or the characters in it, a story that perpetuates feeling sad, victimized, or insufficient, I reframe it to see the growth and to feel empowered and charged up for what is to come next.

What I Hope to Deliver

This book is a retraining guide to life. The chapters of this book are structured like my individual coaching sessions. Within each chapter you will find stories, anecdotes and information explaining each point of the Radical Reframe process as well as a journal exercise and meditation at the conclusion of each chapter. The journaling exercises help us to delve a little deeper into the ideas brought up in each chapter and the meditation works to cultivate awareness around each point. You can read the meditation out loud and record it on your phone or computer to play back and listen to while sitting in a comfortable seat. I don't recommend trying the meditations lying down as most people who are new to meditation will fall asleep. I find doing meditations in a group much more powerful, so perhaps grab some friends or family members to do them with you and then have a discussion afterwards about the experience. In my practice I have been astounded by the experiences of children doing meditation, so you can even make it a family experience.

Some of the exercises will be emotionally difficult, as I will ask you to be very honest with yourself about who you are pretending to be and what you are trying to hide. Just remember that the most painful situations have the most growth potential. As the poet Kahlil Gibran says in his poem *On Pain*, "Your growth is the breaking of the shell that encloses your understanding." When working through these exercises here is a little nugget of truth I have found: it is never as bad as we think it is going to be, and it usually turns out better than we could have imagined. Showing up for yourself is the best gift you can give and embracing the discomfort opens your heart to the possibility of healing. Through this healing, we rewrite our stories.

Are you ready to start unplugging from fear based thinking, judgement and noticing all the things that are not right in your life? Are you ready to start reframing and steering your life in a new direction? A direction that focuses on goals, visions, dreams and all the positive emotions you desire to experience in your day. Well, let's do this!

1

The Radical Reframe Solution: You've got The Power!

*"I've been living on the lip of insanity, wanting to know reasons,
knocking on a door.
It opens. I've been knocking from the inside."*

Rumi

*"What we call our destiny is truly our character and that character can
be altered. The knowledge that we are responsible for our actions and attitudes does not need to be discouraging, because it also means that we are
free to change this destiny."*

Anaïs Nin

The Art of Thinking Differently

*M*any of us have found ourselves at some point feeling as if we have no control over the lives we are living. Clients will explain their unhappiness with statements like "I'm not in love with my husband anymore" or "I hate my job" or "I really want to go back to school" and when questioned why they aren't acting on these feelings I hear "I'm staying with him for the kids" or "I can't afford to leave my job" or "I don't have the resources." I gently remind clients that although they are presenting situations with rationalizations that appear to make perfect sense, they are just reinforcing their belief that they are powerless to change their circumstances. The truth is we always have a choice. It is feeling uncomfortable with unknown consequences that propels us to rationalize why we stay in a life that is not quite painful enough for us to change. This book is a tool to help you understand that you ALWAYS have a choice - unlimited choices, in fact - and the way you choose to see your life dictates how you feel and the path your life will take.

The way we rationalize our inability to act in our lives is through stories. Our lives are permeated with stories. Some stories make us feel good, worthy and loved, others make us feel disempowered, depressed or angry. This book will focus on the disempowering stories we hear and tell ourselves, for they are the ones that are holding us back from the life we want to live. Take a moment to consider all the stories you hear throughout your day. From the grandparent that is forever bemoaning arthritic pain to the girlfriend that is incessantly complaining about her husband. We all are surrounded by people who are eager to share their stories of pain and suffering. Have you ever considered how these stories and the energy with which they are imbued affects your mood and physiology? Have you ever considered that not only do you experience a stream of stories outside of your head, but you also have a continuous narrative running on the inside, too?

Many of us are painfully aware of the stories around us, especially the negative ones that make us feel bad. These are the people we blame for our unhappiness, lack of success or apathy. We often do not take the time to acknowledge how powerful our internal narrative is in influencing our lives. Yet it is often this critical voice which is filled with fear and self-judgment, that truly is shaping what we focus on in our lives. The problem is, unlike the arthritic grandmother or the unhappy girlfriend, our internal thought processes have become so habituated, that they drain our life force without our conscious awareness.

Every situation in our lives has a multitude of interpretations. These different ways of thinking about problems, and challenges can create radically different outcomes, determining whether a situation will feel good or bad, victorious or a great defeat. This is the fundamental principle of reframing. Reframing gives us permission to think differently about ourselves and the problems we are facing by being open to exploring alternative perspectives of the same event, story, or experience, and enabling us to choose a preferred emotional state. This provides a never ending opportunity to choose feeling good no matter what presents before you.

Rhonda's Story

Rhonda had worked for the same medium sized construction company for 20 years and after the unexpected death of her boss, she began to realize the company as she knew it was not going to survive the loss. After watching many of the people she had worked with and cared for deeply over the years be let go from the company, her anxiety increased more and more, until finally she was given her notice. After weeks of contemplating her options, she decided the best thing for her was to sell her house and move closer to her sister and 2 nieces, to be closer to family in case something were to happen where she needed help.

After selling her house and giving away most of her possessions, she moved in with her sister with no idea what to do next. At 61, she felt she would not be considered for open positions as a Corporate Controller, her previous job, and really was not sure she wanted to go back into the corporate environment at all. She was starting to feel that tug that most of us feel at some point in our lives, "what have I really done with my life and now, on the precipice of another chapter, what do I really want to do?" What she loved and really wanted to do was paint. She is a very talented artist, but had never taken the time to develop her skills, and so for much of her life it remained a hobby.

Once settled in Virginia, Rhonda started to look for painting classes and found herself beginning to contemplate going back to school for an art degree. "That is crazy" she would say to herself when telling the story of wanting to go back to school. Besides the fact that she would be a lone baby boomer in a sea of millennials, she also feared the cost and the time, feeling the pinch of being on a retirees' limited budget. After much thought and contemplation, though, she reframed her story and returned to school at age 63. She has never looked back. In her first semester Rhonda enrolled in five art classes. Her family thought she was crazy and setting herself up to fail, but she didn't. Instead, she thrived.

By reframing her notion of what retirement looked like, as well as moving beyond her fears of lack of resources and trusting that if she moved in the direction of her dreams she would be supported, Rhonda is having the time of her life and living her dream. She has befriended the "kids" as she puts it. She springs out of bed each day looking forward to what she is going to learn next and is already planning on getting her masters' degree after she completes her bachelor's degree. Each time she starts to think about money and her fear of not having enough she reframes the thoughts to encompass growth and trust in the process, whatever it ends up looking like.

In the end, Rhonda's financial anxieties were allayed when the faculty awarded her with a $3000 scholarship. All her life Rhonda did what was safe. She worked hard, kept her nose to the grind stone and did what was expected of her because she believed in the story, "life is hard and you have to play it safe." Now, having rewritten her story, she is following her bliss and challenging the old narratives that have held her back most of her life. Rhonda glows with excitement and feels a passion for life she has not felt since she was very young. She has become a role model for her friends, family and the students around her. Rhonda's reframe of retirement has been an inspiration to us all and the energy she exudes for life and learning is completely contagious.

Where We Lose Our Way

Contrary to popular belief, our circumstances do not define our lives. Regardless of what happens to us, we always have the power to choose how we are going to respond to any situation. It's the difference between someone who remains hopeful after being fired from their job and the person who spills coffee on themselves and remains angry for the rest of the day. It all is in how a person perceives their circumstances. The person who is easily pushed into feeling irritable or angry, or has one inconvenient event that colors their entire day, is generally stuck in a pattern of negative story lines. Many of these negative stories about life are called *cognitive distortions*.

The term cognitive distortion is defined as irrational, inflated beliefs that shift a person's perception of reality, usually coloring it in a negative way. Many of these beliefs are automatic thought processes that are so habitual the thinker often does not even realize they have the power to change them and therefore resign themselves to the belief they are powerless to change their circumstances. Because the way a person feels influences how they think, these distorted thoughts can feed negative emotions and lead to an overall negative outlook of the world.

To better explain the value of the reframing process, here are some of the most common cognitive distortions I hear from clients, and a proposed reframe for each. They include *overgeneralizing, catastrophizing, fortune telling, mind reading, martyrdom* and *self-neglect*. See if you can relate to any of the following.

Overgeneralizing draws a conclusion or makes a statement about something that is more general than is justified by the available evidence. For example, when we make a mistake we may exaggerate the consequences of the situation and feel like we are a complete failure. A reframe could be: this mistake is an opportunity for me to learn something new about myself. *Catastrophizing* is closely related to overgeneralizing as we look for or expect the worst-case scenario in a situation, especially in ones where we do not feel confident. I'm reminded of the story of Chicken Little perpetually fearing the sky was falling instead of leaning into his fear and seeing it as an opportunity to prove he can take care of himself and his needs.

Fortune telling involves predicting an specific outcome in the future, when the reality is anything could happen. I have clients who are too afraid to apply for a new job because they fear being rejected. The reframe comes in understanding there is no harm in trying and any effort to change current circumstances will move their life trajectory in a different direction towards what they really want. They may end up in the wrong place for the interview but the right place for the new job or an important chance meeting. *Always* and *never* are usually found within the story of fortune telling; it severely restricts the ability of someone to see alternative endings or the potential for change in people or situations. *Mind reading* closely follows this pattern. It is when we assume we know what other people are thinking or understand their motives without asking. The reverse, expecting people to read our minds, also gets us in trouble. The reframe here is to ask for clarification and state your intentions clearly if things seem vague or misunderstood.

Martyrdom is actively causing suffering within yourself by telling stories of not being appreciated or valued. This is a common pattern in people who take care of others at the expense of their own health and happiness. When these clients complain about being tired or feeling taken advantage of, I recommend a more positive reframe such as, "perhaps when you start to feel worn down or resentful you could see this as a sign that you need to be taking better care of yourself or speaking up for your needs."

Self-neglect is the most destructive story I hear in my office. I frequently hear complaints of weight gain, low energy or sleep loss. When I ask clients why they are not choosing to take better care of themselves, the most common response is, "I don't have time to eat right/exercise/relax." I will gently reframe the story, explaining we all have the same 24 hours in a day, and if you feel you don't have time, you are making other things a priority over self care. This choice is affecting your quality of life. Carving out 15-20 minutes a day for self care is an excellent way of practicing self respect and will affect how you feel about yourself.

Another way in which our stories trap us into one way of seeing things is thinking our stories are absolutely true. This is called black or white thinking, "I am right and you are wrong." A great example of black or white thinking is how we view bugs. Because I was raised with an aversion to bugs, I gag at the thought of eating them. And yet there are people around the world who find chocolate covered grasshoppers a true treat. How can that be true unless there are multiple *true* stories surrounding bugs, and the one I believe is not definitive. I was just brought up with a different story about what is food than someone on the other side of the world who finds deep fried tarantulas delicious. (Yes, that is a true story, my cousin ate one while traveling in Thailand.)

In this example, is there a wrong or a right answer? Of course not. But we have been conditioned to believe that our stories are the right way of seeing things, especially when there is a corresponding emotion or physical reaction behind our beliefs. For example, the queasiness many of us feel when contemplating eating a huge plate of bacon and cheese flavored crickets.

These stories that define our lives and set up the rules of the game, actually box us into a belief system that limits our potential. The tragedy is, we are not taught to question our stories and look outside of the limits of these stories for new possibilities. Without knowing better, we just default to believing that our stories - as distorted as they may be - are true. Rarely do we consider that every day we tell stories to ourselves and others about our highs and lows, heartaches and joys, failures and successes that define the perimeters of how we see our life. Every word you use defines who you are and how you feel. Remember that.

Why Learn The Radical Reframe process?
The Radical Reframe process puts you back in the driver's seat of your life. Reframing offers the freedom to choose how you are going to view a situation rather than feeling trapped by it. The process offers an opportunity to know you are the creator of your own life, and if you don't take responsibility for it, someone else or something else will. It returns the power to you to choose whether you are just having an off day in a

fulfilling life, or believing the forces of the universe are perpetually aligned against you to create a miserable life. It can shift your perspective from the pain you are currently experiencing into an understanding that there is a greater process going on that is preparing you for something good to come. Reframing is a way you can alter your perception of stressors and, thus, relieve significant amounts of angst and anxiety. By actively being curious about your beliefs and reactions, you can surrender judgement of yourself and move towards consciously creating a more positive life: choosing to live within your own chosen stories of heroism, stamina, strength, and support.

Ultimately we have little control over what happens to us but we always have the choice of how to tell the story. It is a powerful realization to know that by changing how we look at things, we see new choices where there were none, possibilities where we felt stuck, power in situations where we felt powerless, and gratitude where we felt over-burdened by worries. This book will give you the tools to shift how you experience each precious moment of your life. By practicing the exercises in this book and learning ways to open your perspective to what is happening around you, you will find you feel more empowered because you know you are in control. Realizing there are nuggets of wisdom and growth in every situation, you will be able to trust whatever comes your way.

This process offers the opportunity to reframe any story that does not feel good, and consequently, shift into a better feeling state. The process of reframing your life begins with the understanding that if you are living a life of pain and suffering you have lost touch with your own personal power. We all experience pain but it does not need to cloud our vision of life and future potential. We lose our personal power many ways: by believing cognitive distortions, allowing toxic people in our lives, doing what we think other people want us to do, feeling it is our job to make people happy, relying on other people for our self esteem, or finally, believing the story that we have no control over what happens to us and how we feel. The problem with this approach to life is that it comes at a cost. Each time we do something based on a desired reaction in our environment or as resistance to what is happening around us, we give up the connection with our inner selves and the peace within and hand it over to other people and external circumstances.

This is an insidious process that becomes so habitual by mid-life that we believe we have little control over what happens to us and feel completely alienated from our passions and desires. We become these passionless robots that are just sleep walking through this thing we call life. Wake up, check. Drink coffee, check. Kids dressed and on the bus, check. Go to work, check. You get the picture. Life becomes a never ending to do list rather than a creative endeavor. This explains why so many of us are willing to spend the bulk of our lives in jobs or marriages, we do not like, or even hate.

The process of getting our power back is about discovering where energy is being lost to external or internal factors, learning to take responsibility for the stories that rationalize these situations and then rewriting the stories to take the energy back. A problem becomes an opportunity, a weakness becomes a strength and a challenge becomes a lesson. Creating a positive reframe for your life offers you room to breathe, grow and feel grateful for whatever circumstances come your way.

The Radical Reframe process changes your brain chemistry for the better. The beauty about reframing is that the brain will follow your self-directed thoughts, as it cannot tell the difference between what is concrete reality and what is created from within. This is why we can get so absorbed in a good movie. The brain believes what it sees, and if the movie is a good one it can convince us that it is real, if only for an hour or two. Even when in *reality* it is just light projecting on a screen.

Your thoughts are just like that movie projector. Imagine the projector is your mind, the film reel is your thoughts and the projected image on the wall is your life. When you run negative reels you get a negative image on the wall. When you run positive reels you get a positive image. It is as simple as that. Your brain responds in kind to the projected image by creating the appropriate chemicals to maintain the mood state you are perpetuating. When we are thinking positive thoughts and exposing ourselves to positive situations we increase levels of available dopamine, serotonin and opiates, and we feel good. When we allow ourselves to be surrounded by negative situations, watch negative television shows or run a stream of negative thoughts through our minds we deplete these feel good chemicals and perpetuate feelings of pain, depression, anger and anxiety. Our thoughts create our reality, and perpetually reinforce it through our brain chemistry.

The final reason you should start practicing Radical Reframing is that the world needs the best version of you to show up. We are living in a world full of negativity. From public shootings, wars on terror, unstable financial markets, and a perceived shortage of time, all of these things which makes us feel isolated and alone. There is plenty to worry about. But does the worry do us any good? I would argue that it does not. Worry does not change a thing but your brain chemistry, creating multiple neural connections that get fired up each time you find something to worry about and this just makes you feel worse.

The solution to this extreme darkness in the world is to add more light. When each of us takes the time to cultivate more positive feelings of love, acceptance and compassion, we become a light for others to do the same. Our task is not to rid the world of it's darkness, but instead to cultivate our own inner light until we shine so brightly that the darkness is enveloped and transformed. The world desperately needs your light and you deserve it. Marianne Williamson says it nicely, "As we let our own light shine, we unconsciously give other people permission to do the same." Reframing is about learning to trust the process of your own life and knowing you can never get it wrong, that no matter what appears before you, you can handle it, you can grow from it and you can be happy.

Freedom from Stinking Thinking
As a psychiatric physician assistant, I make a living prescribing medications that alter a person's biochemistry. Or as one of my therapist co-workers put it, I am a glorified drug dealer. In many ways this is true, through my profession I have the ability to artificially alter a person's biochemistry, in the hope of offering a temporary reprieve from a certain mood state. I like to think I offer more than just drugs, though, as

I try to challenge the belief patterns that reinforce an unwanted mood state. Until people are willing to look at and change the underlying stories they tell themselves over and over, they will continue to see only the problems in their world and not the solutions. With or without medication. That is why I am writing this book.

In my office I educate people on how they can alter their own biochemistry through diet, exercise and brain health, but many report they do not have the time or money to invest in such practices. This book will help you to utilize the fastest way I know to affect your biochemistry and support a happy, healthy brain. It is free and available to all. All you need is a strong commitment to be willing to change, an open mind and some time to practice being mindful.

Reframing your stories is the place to start. Stories are the foundation for how you view everything that happens to you. Every thought, if consistently repeated, creates a neural connection that evolves into a pattern of association that continues into a habit form. The more emotionally charged a thought is, the stronger and quicker a connection is created. Think a thought often enough and the neural connection will get strong, your brain cells literally create a social club around the thought making multiple connections and relationships that make the thought easy to trigger and associate with the things going on in your life. When you think the thought, your cells have a biochemical party, releasing neurotransmitters that recreate the familiar feeling associated with that thought.

We literally become addicted to our mood states by this process. Conversely, if a thought has no emotional charge or is rarely stimulated, relationships between the cells become loose or are never created. Even if in the past something did cause a strong emotional response, if we work to reduce the pull of the reaction through mindfulness, those neural connections will wither away from disuse and the thought will eventually cease to have an effect on our physiology.

A good example of reframing most of us can relate to is where our thoughts go when we believe someone is being rude to us. Do you immediately get irritable and behave rudely back, do you collapse into self-blame, wondering what you could have done to elicit this behavior, or do you have compassion for the person and send them a prayer of love? The negative reactions you may have to this person are just habituated biochemical reactions to a pattern recognition that you have defined as rude. If you in any way push back in a negative manner you are perceiving the behavior personally as intended mistreatment towards you. The reality of the situation is most behaviors other people engage in have nothing to do with us.

As in the example above, if someone is being rude, perhaps they are worried about a sick child they had to leave at home to come to work, or don't have enough money to pay their rent this month, or suffer from depression. Perhaps someone was just rude to them. If we take their behavior personally it becomes our problem and is reflective of the story we tell ourselves about the situation. When we learn to not take things so personally, make it a habit to assume the best of those around us and wish each person well, we are actively ensuring we stay in a positive state of mind. And we might even help the other person wake up from the fugue of their story and choose better thoughts. Emotions are contagious: being mindful of yours helps set into motion more kindness and compassion in the world.

Journaling 101

As we begin this journey, I would encourage you to start keeping a thought journal and begin writing down difficult situations and relationships. Journals are helpful tools for many reasons. By writing down situations and your feelings about them you can start to see where your thoughts go in different situations and begin to recognize patterns in your stories. It also is helpful to start charting your mood state. You may notice you feel more anxious at the end of the work day or irritable after spending 4 hours doing house work. Writing things down presents the opportunity to reflect on situations and review our emotional reactions after having had time to calm down and have the gift of distance. Putting our initial thoughts down on paper makes it very real and helps us to see just how lost in stories we can become when we get emotionally triggered, tired or frustrated. You can begin to see where you are getting stuck in self defeating beliefs and patterns and with the gift of time, you can begin to tease out the facts from fiction to create a new story that will catapult you towards where you want to be. Lastly, it gives us an opportunity to rewrite the story in a more supportive and helpful fashion that promotes self compassion and acceptance.

Here is a simple template to start with as you begin journaling your stories. I would recommend you leave a page or two after each entry so you can go back and rewrite the situation after you have calmed down to start playing with the reframe process.

1. When you find yourself triggered, write out the situation with as much detail as possible. Just let your mind go and write down whatever thoughts come to you no matter how negative. Remember, if you are not honest with how you are thinking with yourself you can't begin to change the patterns, so just let it all go and really get to the bottom of how you are feeling and the story you are telling.

2. After you have exhausted the initial flow of energy, put the journal aside. Go do something else and come back a few hours or days later, once the emotional reaction has subsided. Ask yourself what the initial reaction was that you had to this situation. Write it down below the story. This is where we begin to see the unfolding of the unconscious story, the prominent pattern that has been shaping your life. As you reread the story, write down the highlights that you see in the story and its themes. Some examples would be: feeling victimized, powerless, abused or taken advantage of, worthless, unlovable, not smart enough, criticized or not being supported.

3. Consider each highlight and ask where that belief might be coming from. For example, did your father always feel he was being cheated by someone? Or was your mother always feeling victimized by people? Was your family poor which caused you to feel different from the other kids at school, or could you never shine

next to your sibling's accomplishments? Consider where you started believing that this story was true.

4. Try to take a step back from the story and see the situation from a different persons' perspective, or imagine you were observing as a third party. How does a shift in perspective change the story? Literally imagine someone else interpreting the situation and how they might comment on your reaction.

5. Create a positive belief or affirmation in response to your reconsideration of the situation. For instance, if you felt victimized, write down a statement about being strong. If you felt criticized, write a statement about trying your best. Write down a statement that reflects a healthier interpretation of the situation.

6. Rewrite the story with a positive spin, using your imagination and humor to reframe the story and then let it go. Remember, this is a practice, and as you intend more and more to understand your stories and reactions, this intention will cultivate a greater awareness of your life and how you perpetuate the stories with your beliefs. With practice, I promise the shift will come, and with it a profound opening into self awareness that is the key to reframing your life.

Don't worry if this feels a little overwhelming or awkward at first, we will add bits and pieces to the journaling process along the way so that by the time we are done you will be a pro. For now the most important thing is to start catching yourself when you get emotional and writing it down. We have to catch these stories while we are creating them to cultivate awareness of the process. The ego is slick and tricks us into believing that our stories are real, so writing it down is the best skill you have for starting to get honest with yourself.

Our initial reactions are like well-trodden landscaped paths of lifeless dirt that are constantly being pruned. Each time we think a habituated thought such as, my boss is a jerk or I'm an idiot, we are reinforcing the comfort of that thought by walking down the familiar path, even if in the long run the thought pattern causes us pain. This is why our habitual thoughts are so easy to access. When we are creating new pathways, such as "my boss has high expectations" or "I don't quite understand this information," at first it can be challenging to access these new stories as the path does not currently exist; it is covered in brambles and weeds, completely unfamiliar to us. And so, just like developing a new skill or strengthening a muscle, it takes time and patience to create a new neural pathway. But take heart, anyone can do it!

Meditation 101

Meditation is one of the best gifts we can give ourselves to create a sense of calm, peace and balance that benefits both our emotional well-being and overall health. With practice, just a few breaths and directed thoughts can soothe anxiety and calm down a restless mind. As with all meditations, you need to practice during quiet times in your life in order for it to become a useful tool in times of stress. Clients will often start trying a recommended meditation in the midst of complete chaos and wonder why it did not help. Meditation is like a muscle, and we have to start strengthening it with practice while we are relaxed before we can begin to call on the strength of the skill when things are falling apart.

Try to let go of judgement if you have a hard time focusing on the meditation. It is the nature of the mind to wander; creating mindful focus takes practice. Just imagine you are strengthening the muscle of your brain. Once you have practiced conditioning this muscle, you will have a very powerful tool in your toolbox to help you reframe your perceptions. For when things start to get stressful, just do your favorite meditation from this book and your body/mind goes "Yes, I remember this and when we do this we feel relaxed and can let go."

Your nervous system will consequently relax reflexively as neuro-chemicals are released because of your practice. Once you are in a more relaxed state, you are free to see whatever is bothering you more clearly while reworking the story. Please do yourself a favor and practice, practice, practice. Most of the meditations in this book can be done in less than 10 minutes, and this one in particular can take literally 2 minutes once you have it down.

Another thing to keep in mind with meditation is that you cannot do it wrong and everyone can do it. I promise. Just keep coming back to your "mat" as we say in yoga, the proverbial sacred space, and you will develop your own meditation style. When doing the meditations in this book I would recommend recording yourself saying the meditation and then listen to it while you sit quietly. Relax and allow yourself to guide you back to center.

Heart Meditation

Sit in a comfortable chair with a back, and allow your body to begin to soften and be supported by the chair. Make any adjustments so you feel supported and comfortable. Notice your breath, watching it come and go, in and out. Allow your body to breathe and gently observe your body responding to your breath.

Begin imagining on the in breath drawing in a golden light that fans throughout your body and on the out breath inviting your body to release any tightness, negativity, or self-judgement. Allow yourself to be soothed by your breath, feeling the movement of the breath like waves moving to and from from the shoreline. The golden light is like an elixir, soothing any rough spots and helping the body to relax. Continue doing this for a few moments, until you feel your body begin to soften and let go.

Once relaxed, take both hands and gently drape them over the center of your chest, your heart chakra. Allow them to rest here as you breathe, feeling your hands rise and fall with the breath. Feel the warmth and gentle pressure of the hands on your chest as you bring awareness to this space in your body. Give your heart permission to soften with each breath.

Bring to mind someone that you love very much. This person may be alive now, or they may be deceased. It should be someone who elicits a positive feeling of support and love. Grandparents are an easy pick, but if you did not have a good relationship with your grandparents or did not know them, and no one else comes to mind, call upon an angel, spirit guide or even your higher self.

As you invite in an energy of love and acceptance, imagine this person is coming up behind you and enveloping you in their arms. Feel the warmth of their embrace and imagine they are radiating unconditional love and grace, and directing it towards you. Sit for a few moments soaking in the warmth of the love, staying connected to your breath. Imagine with each in breath you are drawing in a feeling of love and support into your body and infusing every cell with this feeling. Each time you breathe out invite your body to let go of any fear, anxiety, negativity or judgement.

Once you feel the negative energy has shifted, allow your hands to return to your lap, release the image and come back into awareness of your breathing. Feeling yourself sitting on the chair, become aware of the sounds in the room. Begin moving your fingers and toes, gently waking up the body. When you are ready, open your eyes and continue on with your day. As you go through your day, periodically take a minute to touch back in with your heart and reconnect with that feeling of love in your chest. The more effort you put into cultivating this feeling of connection with the heart and love feeling the easier it will become for you to reframe negative stories and create more positive ones.

Take Home Message

Are you ready to start learning how to reframe your life? If you have done the exercises in this chapter, good for you for making the first step. I would encourage you to practice the heart meditation every day, it is a powerful tool to connect with your inner self and cultivate self-compassion. While many people understand the heart is a physical organ that pumps blood throughout the body, few are aware that the heart is an information processing center with its own nervous system, hormones, and a direct line to the brain that influences our perception, decision making, and other cognitive processes.

Developing a conscious relationship with your heart is the beginning of a life-long friendship. Heart centered people live longer, are less stressed, are more flexible and have a stronger sense of identity and security. As we develop our connection to our hearts, our hearts begin to speak to us and point out what is really important in life. Through physical sensations and intuitive hits, your heart will start giving you clues for when you are in alignment with your higher self or falling off the path into stories of disempowerment. Your heart is your primary ally in reframing self-judgement and negativity to embracing self-love and compassion. It is the place I go every time I hear the negative self-talk in my head start to ramp up. It is the quickest route to reframe my stories.

Now that you have been introduced to the power of heart-centered awareness, we will move into a deeper awareness of your physical being and surroundings. There are so many benefits to a mindfulness practice I could fill a book with them alone, but here are just a few: it helps relieve stress, improves heart disease, lowers blood pressure, reduces chronic pain, improves sleep, increases emotional resilience, enhances feelings of happiness, and deepens our connection with ourself and others. In the next chapter we will be taking the awareness you cultivated in this chapter even deeper, to encompass your entire being. Buckle your seat belt. You are about to get an invitation to wake up from this dream called life.

2

Awareness: Waking up from the Dream

"I've worked all my life on the subject of awareness, whether it's awareness of the body, awareness of the mind, awareness of your emotions, awareness of your relationships, or awareness of your environment. I think the key to transforming your life is to be aware of who you are."

Deepak Chopra

"Have you ever had a dream, Neo, that you were so sure was real? What if you were unable to wake from that dream, Neo? How would you know the difference between the dream world and the real world?"

Morpheus in *The Matrix*

Human beings have an amazing capacity for compassion, love, and humility, as well as a deep-seated need for connection. Yet in our ever-evolving technological age, we seem to be moving away from this instinctive essence of our being, towards a life of automated behaviors and emotional isolation. Our times of genuine connection through a dinner table conversation or a long walk with a friend have been replaced with texting and Facebook. How did this become the norm of human interactions?

I will admit that technology is transforming our lives and shaping the future in many incredible ways, yet it comes at a profound cost to the individual. In our "culture of distraction" many of us are finding ourselves living with divided attentions and depleted energy resources. Most of us live on the hamster wheel of "more, better, faster" and find we do not know how to get off. We are always busy, and the result in our lives is stress. Stress that presents in a variety of ways: irritability, anxiety, unhealthy diets, poor sleep habits, not exercising regularly, making hasty (and usually, poor) decisions and feeling generally unsatisfied with life.

This chapter will introduce you to the art of dropping back into your life through mindful awareness. This *dropping in* as I call it, is a simple yet life-altering practice that will help you to build a stronger relationship with yourself and those around you. With self awareness we are able to know who we truly are. We can identify our strengths and weaknesses, as well as our needs and desires, and proceed with this information to guide us into creating lives full of honesty, love and passion. This greater self-knowledge not only enables us to better support ourselves and others, but to be more present and aware of how our choices affect our lives. It is the starting point for finding balance in this ever unbalanced world of do, do, do. Awareness is the best place to start to begin reframing your life, as it starts with YOU!

How Awareness Radically Changed My Life

Through most of my life I have suffered from severe asthma. At the age of 1 years old, I became very sick and was initially diagnosed with Cystic Fibrosis. A definitive diagnosis of asthma soon followed. Plagued by frequent lung and sinus infections, I was fed a steady diet of antibiotics and steroids through out my childhood and frequently found myself in the ER being pumped full of epinephrine. My disease peaked at age 27 and 28, when I had two 10-day stays in the hospital with life-threatening asthma attacks. I distinctly remember during this time asking God to just please let me die, because I was so miserable. My request went unheeded, though, and I survived to be even more petrified of my illness and my inability to control it.

My relationship to asthma was radically reframed while working with Gabrielle, my first breath meditation teacher. Gabrielle was a yoga instructor who incorporated a lot of Breathwork in her classes. Her breathing exercises were helpful in managing my anxiety, and I sought her help when I was planning my wedding. We worked together for several months, leading up to, and through, my wedding date. The breath mindfulness practices not only helped immensely with my anxiety, but they also helped with something else I did not expect.

When I was on my honeymoon it occurred to me that I had no idea where my inhaler was. Not only had I not packed it, but I could not remember the last time I used it. Here I was nine months into practicing breath awareness and completely unaware of the location of my "emergency" inhaler because I had not had an emergency in months. This was amazing considering how stressed I had been over the prior nine months moving back to Virginia, planning a wedding, and beginning a new career. In the past I had always observed a relationship between my breathing and stress levels. The more stressed I was, the more likely I was to develop restricted breathing, followed by lung and/or sinus infections. Breathwork taught me an awareness of my body to the point that I unconsciously began to circumvent my asthma attacks altogether.

With full awareness of the messages my lungs are sending me, I now know well before my breathing becomes labored that my body is sending signs to pay attention and increase my self-care. In her book, *You Can Heal Your Life*, Louise Hay explains the lungs represent grief, depression and a fear of taking in life. I pay attention to this message now, when I feel that gentle tickle in my lungs, or begin to have the slightest whisper of breathlessness after going up a flight of stairs: I stop and drop into awareness of my being. I immediately slow down, cut back on my schedule, take lots of epsom salt baths, and pull out the essential oils to increase my self care. I then go inward and explore the emotional messages my lungs are trying to send me. This practice has been life-changing. Thanks to the awareness which Breathwork gave me, I am essentially "cured" of a disease that once threatened to take my life. That is the power of mindful awareness; it will change your life, I guarantee it.

Waking up From the Dream of Doing

Have you ever considered the question: *are you living or being lived?* What is it to be a "human doing" rather than a "human being?" In the ever increasing pressures of modern day life, many of us have lost touch with what really matters to us and who we really are. We have shifted our definition of success from peace within to success without and have completely lost touch with what it means to *just be.*

In many ways we have become *the walking unaware.* We are woefully unaware of the messages our bodies send us. We have no idea what our emotions mean and fail to pay attention to our reactions to things. Ultimately we give little thought to how our beliefs and stories shape our lives. This in large part due to the fact that technology has become a filter, screening out an authentically lived experience, and instead, supplanting a surreal alter reality that we are all trying to acquire.

A great example is Facebook. Clients repeatedly tell me how they feel isolated and depressed after spending time on Facebook, yet can't seem to disengage. It is like a drug, a compulsion to witness all that we are not experiencing, and then beating ourselves up for the shortcomings we believe we have in our own lives. The assumption is all the smiling happy people we see have perfect lives. Rationally we know this is not true, but the story-making machine of an unchecked brain will believe it. If I challenge clients and ask, "do you really believe that the people who are only posting fun happy pictures truly have perfect lives?" Most will reply "no, they don't, but it feels that way when I am on Facebook." That is the power of an unconscious story: it can be completely irrational and untrue, but if left unchallenged, it can dramatically affect a person's disposition for a day, or week, or even a lifetime.

The first step in reframing your life is starting to drop back into what it feels like to be a human being having an authentic human experience which involves reconnecting with the messages of your body, emotions and thoughts. There are so many variables in life that we have little control over, and this skill of *being* helps us to accept whatever is going on around us, assess how we got there and then gives us the peace of mind to effectively deal with life's challenges rather than being bowled over by them.

When we become disconnected from the quality of being, we lose touch with our passion and desires. We end up feeling untethered and tossed around by life circumstances because we have lost trust in our own inner wisdom and intuition. Practicing mindful awareness reconnects you with yourself, your emotions, your environment, your fellow human beings, and with a higher sense of purpose. If we desire to live in a place of contentedness, we must learn to move out of the dream of doing and start living in the reality of the human experience. Only then can we consciously move from collapsing into a story of shortcomings and "don't haves" into a reframe of where you truly want to live. We shift out of a belief that we must *do* to be happy, into an understanding that the joy is in the awareness of being, and being able to consciously create a narrative that supports this flow.

Cultivating Mindful Awareness

Psychologist Daniel Goleman, author of the best selling book, *Emotional Intelligence*, (Bantam Books, 2005) has proposed a definition of self-awareness as "knowing one's internal states, preferences, resources and intuitions." This definition places an emphasis on the ability to monitor our inner world of bodies, thoughts and emotions as they arise. This awareness, which is also referred to as mindfulness, offers us the opportunity to connect with our internal world and how we interface with the outside world. Mindful awareness has been proven to reduce stress, boost working memory, improve focus and concentration, decrease emotional reactivity, enhance communication skills and create a better quality of life. I don't know about you, but all of that sounds really good to me, and all we have to do is just start paying attention to what is really going on both inside and outside of ourselves.

Becoming aware of your unconscious thoughts and emotions can be scary. Most of us have spent a lifetime running away from them. Few of us were taught how to name and process our feelings, and therefore have become masters of diversion, denial and avoidance. But the rewards of taking responsibility for your thoughts and feelings are well worth it. I promise. As you begin to observe how you act out in your life -- pinpoint when you blame yourself or others or try to rationalize away a behavior -- you give yourself permission to just *be*. You will begin to soften towards your self, recognizing you are doing your best and that is enough. In this softening towards your self you will also be able to give permission to other's to be who they are without trying to change them. Mindful awareness helps us to understand ourselves, but also understand human nature, and to learn to see that we are all in this together.

Awareness is a skill we can cultivate and as we do, we begin to understand we are not defined by our thoughts and judgments. We are something much greater and deeper: beings with truly unlimited possibility. Unfortunately, most of us were never taught this truth. Instead we were raised with messages that we are less than perfect, need to do something to be of value and that there is much to fear in life. We internalized these messages which in turn became the stories we tell ourselves repeatedly to explain our current circumstances. "It is because I am not _____." You can fill in the blank with your favorite deficiency: not smart enough, thin enough, rich enough, witty enough, the list goes on. But the truth of the matter is the same. None of these stories are true, they are just that: stories. They are self-sabotaging beliefs that you picked up at some point and allowed to become a part of your identity and therefore turned your power over to these beliefs to shape your current life circumstances.

Separating Fact from Fiction
The first step of cultivating mindful awareness is separating this long-standing fiction of self limiting stories from the facts. The fictional component of our lives is the meaning and stories we attribute to our experiences; the facts are what is actually happening. During a session, my client Molly went on a rampage about her husband's affair, and how

she found his deception to be devastating. Tearful and distraught, she repeatedly asked me, "How could this be happening?" When I asked how she found out about the affair, Molly said she did not know for sure, she just had a feeling something was going on. I challenged her to look at how much distress she was causing herself by making up a story that she did not know to be true. Why not ask her husband so she could know the truth and stop living in a state of fear? She reported she was too afraid to ask because she feared it might be true. So, instead of honoring her intuition and respecting herself by asking for clarity, Molly chose to lose herself in the abyss of what if, creating a perpetual state of anxiety for which she was asking me to prescribe medication to alleviate her discomfort. Although she may have been correct in her assessment, she was wasting a lot of time and energy making up a story without knowing the facts.

The Radical Reframe process starts with cultivating awareness of what your life feels like to you *right now*. Time and again, I see clients who spend a great deal of energy avoiding how they really feel and blaming other people and situations for why they feel so bad. I'll ask: "how does that make YOU feel?" In return I am met with that blank stare, as if I asked if they believed in aliens. So this is where our work begins, at the edge of the abyss of not knowing what it feels like to be a human being, with all our faults and vulnerabilities. We will be cultivating an awareness of the body, then move into our mind, and thoughts, and how they interact to create an image of reality.

Your Body as a Messenger

Our bodies are amazingly complex biological systems that function as the container of our human form. They are the mediator between our internal landscape and the external world. The information we glean from our senses comes in at lightening speed, travels through fibrous units called nerves up our spine and into our brain to be processed almost immediately within the most advanced supercomputer on earth: our brains.

Cultivating nonjudgmental awareness toward our bodies helps foster greater self-acceptance, internal peace and helps us to trust the process of living in these gifts called bodies. We learn to appreciate our bodies more for what they are, what they do, and what they make possible, and we learn to let go of the constant judgment and social comparison of what our bodies are not. When you become more aware of your body and its sensations, you become more likely to notice stress, discomfort, and tension. Body awareness gives you the head's up when it might be time to step back, take a break and not over work yourself. When you're hungry, you know it's time to eat. When you're full, you know it's time to stop. When you're tired, you know it's time to take a break. And yet, how many of us feel we flow fluidly through each of these processes? How good are you at recognizing what your body needs?

Practicing mindful breathing is a natural place to start cultivating awareness of the body. Breathing is one of the few autonomic functions of the nervous system that we can easily access and control, thereby making it a good entry point into learning awareness of the body. The autonomic nervous system is a branch of the nervous system that acts largely unconsciously and regulates bodily functions such as heart rate, digestion, respiratory rate and elimination. The autonomic nervous system has two branches: the sympathetic nervous system and the parasympathetic nervous system. The sympathetic nervous system is often considered the "fight or flight" system, while the parasympathetic nervous system is often considered the "rest and digest" system.

In many cases, these systems have opposing actions: one system activates a physiological response and the other inhibits it. We can use this to our advantage. When we feel stressed or anxious, meaning we are in a sympathetic state of being, we can consciously slow down and deepen our breathing to shift into the more relaxed state of parasympathetic relaxation. Like magic, our heart rates will slow down, our blood pressure lowers, and we will start to release tension that has built up in our muscles. It is as easy as that.

Take a moment to become aware of how you are sitting right at this moment. Are you sitting up straight or are you slouched over? I would like for you to do a quick experiment. Start slouching really far down in your seat. Take a minute to notice how this posture affects how you feel. Notice your breathing and how restricted it becomes in this posture. When we slouch we compress the lower lobes of the lungs, thereby significantly reducing surface area for oxygen to diffuse into the blood and carbon dioxide and toxins to diffuse out. Reduced oxygen not only causes us to feel lethargic and tired, but also contributes to issues we may have with focus and concentration. Slouching also reduces circulation of the blood through out the abdomen and up into the brain. This posture has been proven to increase negative thinking and create a depressed mood. Check in with how you feel emotionally: are you down, tired, or depressed? Now think about how often you slouch in your life: in your car, while eating, at work, while on the computer. Modern humans "doing" spend most of their day slouched over something, and if you are not bringing awareness to this fact you are not only adversely affecting your body and health, but also perpetuating a negative mood state.

Now I want you to sit up straight. Really pull the top of your head towards the ceiling, roll your shoulders back and poke your chest out. Now notice how your breath feels. Notice how your belly is open and your neck is up straight, as the lungs are fully able to fill completely with oxygen. Knowing that your blood is now fully able to flow to your brain and belly. Take a few moments to notice how you feel. Lighter, stronger, happier? I would ask you to take it a little further and just raise your arms towards the sky and then extend them out like you were going to try to hug the sun. Now breathe and notice how your breath and body feel. Once your arms tire, release them but keep sitting upright and just breathe for a few more moments. Not only does good posture ensure proper oxygenation and blood flow, but an upright posture supports self confidence, a better mood, and increased focus and concentration.

Here is a body awareness challenge. Put a timer on your phone to go off every hour for a whole day. When the timer goes off, get up and stretch for a minute or two, touch your toes, stretch your calves, anything to open up your body. After doing this 8 to10 times through out the day, notice how your day went and how your body feels. Most clients report feeling more energetic and upbeat by the end of the day. Challenge a friend to do this exercise with you and compare notes. I find that if I start to stretch when my body feels tight, it wants more. This is a good way to start an exercise regimen, with just 10 minutes every day. Try it. You might like it.

Body Language

Have you ever considered how people read your body language? Have you thought about how your body language affects your mood? We communicate a lot through our posture, gestures, and facial expressions. In fact some researchers believe we communicate more through our non-verbal gestures than we do with our words. When you improve your body awareness, and begin to notice more how you are holding your body in space, you become aware of the signals you are sending to yourself and out to others.

Our body language also affects neurochemistry. A great example is smiling. Smiling is contagious: seeing a smiling person makes you want to smile too, and as a result you will feel better, even if you were not feeling particularly happy before the encounter. The act of smiling releases a neurotransmitter in the brain called dopamine. Dopamine is a reward chemical because it brings us the feeling of pleasure; it is released every time we do something pleasurable such as eating chocolate, laughing with friends, or having sex. Dopamine is one of the primary chemicals involved in the development of addictions because once we feel the influence of its reward, we want more and more.

Let's do an experiment. First I want you to take a minute and sit with your eyes closed and frown. Really pull the sides of your lips down and sit there feeling how it makes you feel. Does your face respond to the frown, do you find your brow furrows, or your eyes squint? Take a moment to sit like this and see how the frown affects your mood. Do you feel more tired, irritable or sad? Now let's turn it around and make yourself smile. It can be a big Christmas morning smile or a little Mona Lisa smile, either one works. Just sit here for a minute with your eyes closed and smile. What happened? Every time, I start feeling better, lighter and thinking happy thoughts. What did you notice?

I would challenge you to do an experiment with smiling. Mark a day on your calendar as "my happy day" and commit for one day to smile at every person you see. It will feel uncomfortable at first because generally when we smile at other people it is because we expect a positive response, but go out on a limb today and just let the smiles flow. The responses alone will make you laugh, as some people will ignore you, some will shrug the smile off, but others will genuinely smile back and that really feels good. When it happens I encourage you to feel where it hits in your body, most likely it will be your heart space, smack in the center of your chest. I did this exercise the other day at the airport, truly a place of misery, and one lady said out of the blue, "You go Girl." That made my day, all because I turned that frown upside down.

The Software of Your Brain

According to Wikipedia, reality is "the state of things as they actually exist, rather than as they appear or might be imagined." It is interesting to ponder how we might really know what is reality for it is almost impossible for us to know what is truly real, as every experience we have is being translated through the interface of our brain and senses. We each have a very different brain based on many variables, including our genes, the quality of our diet, the complexity of our social network, and the circumstances of our childhood, just to name a few. Mindful awareness helps us to see with greater clarity the reality of what is happening in front and inside of us, giving us the opportunity to start to tease out our perceptions from what is really happening. Before we move onto awareness of the brain and thoughts, I think it is important to understand a little about how your brain responds to the outside world.

I explain the biology of the brain to clients as follows. This is my beginner's guide to neuroanatomy, which I believe gives clients a good basis to understand what is going on between their ears. The limbic system is a part of the middle brain, and for the purposes of my coaching practice, I am concerned with two functions of the middle brain: emotional regulation and the fight or flight system. As information arrives to the spinal column, the nervous system determines if the body is in physical danger or not, even before the sensory stimulation has been registered in the brain. For example, if you touch a hot burner you will move your hand immediately based on a reflex coming from the spinal column before the information fully reaches and is processed by the brain that you have been burned. This is a protective mechanism of the brain to avoid harm. This is why when something feels, tastes, sounds or looks funny we will initially react to a potential danger: we react before the situation has been fully processed.

When information does reach the brain, it is screened through our mid brain, our fight or flight center, to determine the level of danger a situation might involve. You may have experienced entering a room and feeling the hairs stand up on the back of your neck, not understanding why, and then experience the exact same feeling when you bend to pet a dog and it emits a low, almost inaudible growl. The limbic system goes into alert mode whether or not you have consciously registered a definitive threat. Regardless the brain is sending you a message.

Have you ever been in a situation where you have a strong emotional reaction that is completely out of proportion to the situation at hand? Well, this is your middle brain too, hijacking your brain because it has made an assumption of what was going on based on past experiences; your limbic system was perceiving a threat of some kind that was out of proportion to the reality of the situation. Because we are wired for survival, our brains will automatically over generalize a stimulus if it in any way is reminiscent of a past danger or hurtful experience. With this overgeneralization comes a type of snowball effect that will run out of control if we are not mindful of our reactions.

When we become alarmed, a series of neurochemical reactions occur, priming the body to fight, fright, or flee. The limbic system produces hormones which stimulate the release of catecholamines, especially norepinephrine, epinephrine and cortisol. When we experience a heightened emotional reaction our bodies respond with a dramatic dumping of these chemicals into our blood stream that cause heart rates to increase, lungs to expand, and blood pressure to go up. We access the sympathetic nervous system so we are ready to act fast in case of danger.

The key point to remember here is that the mind is *unaware of what is real or not real; it cannot tell the difference between a perceived versus a real threat, and will sound the alarm for both.* I would venture to say that 99% of the time we go into this sympathetic overdrive mode, we are in fact completely safe. This is often what is going on in the body when people suffer from anxiety; their brains are constantly reacting to perceived threats that are locked in the brain from the past but most often are not threatening in the present moment.

Chronic anxiety is a situation when the limbic system gets stuck in overdrive. This is why when we are anxious we have a hard time concentrating or remembering things: when people tell us to "snap out of it!" we can't, because we are lost in an irrational red alert mode. I tell clients when you are running from the proverbial saber tooth tiger, you don't need to be figuring out calculus. Meaning, when your brain senses danger, whether real or not, you go into fight or flight mode and lose your rational upper level brain processing abilities. Mindfulness helps us to see when we are moving into an assumption of danger. We learn to use anxiety as a signal to calm the body, regain control of the internal situation, and then calmly look to see what might be triggering us.

If the brain determines a situation is safe, we can begin to process how we feel about the current events. If we are not practicing conscious awareness as feelings arise, the brain will assign them a meaning based on a reservoir of past experiences. Have you ever heard someone say, "why does this always happen to me?" It is because they keep assigning the same meaning to different situations that arouse a similar emotion. As an example, take the friend who always seems to pick boyfriends who cheat. This individual *unconsciously* recognizes a familiar pattern, and gets caught up in playing out the same dynamic time and again. This friend forgets or denies how painful the outcome often is because the familiarity of the situation is almost addictive. Without conscious awareness we will continue to pick what is familiar, even if the familiar hurts.

Further complicating this situation is that most often - while well intentioned - our parents did not teach us how to process our emotions in a healthy manner. We received messages of "don't cry," "you're fine," and "don't make this a big deal," instead of encouragement to explore our internal landscapes and learn to acknowledge our feelings and administer self care. So many of us are simply wounded children walking around in adult bodies with no understanding of how we are feeling or how to process our emotions. This is often what leads to out of control emotional reactions such as anger and anxiety as well as the very immature habit of blaming.

My client Melissa came to me for help with her escalating anxiety. After a few sessions it became clear that a large part of her anxiety was coming from her marriage. She was having problems with her husband and considering leaving him. As we explored her past, we discovered she was from a "no talk" family that made fun of anyone who expressed their emotions. The messages Melissa got about feelings were as follows: hide them at all costs because if they were expressed it would lead to pain and ridicule. Before working with me, when a difficult situation would arise, Melissa would ignore it because she was never taught how to work through her feelings. What she did learn was when her emotions were triggered her middle brain went into high alert waiting for threats of ridicule and shame, which meant she experienced anxiety, and a lot of it.

When she and her husband would have problems, Melissa would withdraw emotionally and her husband would feel frustrated. This was not a productive behavior when trying to resolve a conflict. With the help of individual coaching, and some sessions with her husband, Melissa was able to begin to see that her emotions were not dangerous. She began to see that her anxiety was coming from the act of hiding of her emotions and the belief that expressing them was dangerous. When Melissa was able to trust herself and her husband with her emotions, her anxiety slowly began to wane. With time she learned to trust herself with her feelings and how to appropriately express them to her husband. Once she was able to give words to her feelings and trust herself and her husband to care for them, her anxiety lessened and her marriage improved.

The Placebo Effect

The human mind is so powerful that our thoughts alone have been proven to affect bodily processes. Individuals who experience persistent depression, stress and sadness often suffer from a weakened immune system and a wide range of health problems, including heart disease, chronic pain and high blood pressure. Thoughts are powerful. Most of us have heard of "the placebo effect": the health-inducing effect people experience when they believe they're getting a helpful drug or treatment but are actually getting no treatment at all. The placebo effect is real and it's not just in your head: it actually can dilate bronchi, heal ulcers, make warts disappear, resolve headache pain, and drop blood pressure all through the power of suggestion. Positive thoughts can create the same healing effects in your body. A daily practice of mindful meditation, which helps us to disengage from our thoughts, has been known to reduce stress, increase relaxation and enhance a general sense of well-being. Meditation lowers the heart rate and blood pressure, increases focus and attention, and reduces cortisol levels, which are stress hormones that can harm your body. All this comes from taking just a few minutes a day to pay attention to yourself.

I encourage you to pay attention to your thoughts and reactions throughout the course of your day. When you experience stress or frustration, ask yourself what thoughts you are having in reaction to the situation at hand. If negative thoughts or judgments arise, try to replace them with something more neutral or positive: inserting appreciation, gratitude or just changing the subject. The more we practice mindful awareness, the better we get at catching ourselves in self defeating body postures or stinking thinking. Mindful awareness frees us to create a more positive outlook that shines from within.

Journal: Write your own Manifesto

We cultivate self-awareness with the hope of improving ourselves and our lives. With this in mind, it is helpful to set some personal goals and push yourself to figure out what you want out of life. In the spirit of shifting your neurochemistry to create more positive mood states, I want you to write your own manifesto. The manifesto is a motivational declaration of intent. It should include what is most important to you and reflect the person you aspire to be.

A manifesto can have multiple functions. It is a statement of principles, a rebellious call to action, and an invitation to help you connect with the authentic you. You can create a manifesto that encompasses your life desires or you can create individualized manifestos for specific areas of your life: some examples might be work, relationships, and parenting. I would recommend starting with no more than three manifestos so you do not feel overwhelmed.

Here is my work Manifesto. I read it everyday before I start seeing clients.

> *Divine Spirit,*
> *Please help me to remember that each person who comes to me today is in pain and seeking comfort and guidance. May I see each of them as a human being with the same needs and desires as me: to feel loved, accepted and healthy. May my words lift their hearts and give them solace and hope. May I infuse with each word I use and each prescription I write the intention of health and healing, and may I wish each person who comes through my office door the opportunity to experience Divine health. May I help each client to see they have the power to create the life they want. May I be of service with a heart full of gratitude.*
> *Namaste.*

You may find you are surprised at what starts to come up as you delve into what you really want to create in your life. Manifesto creation is a wonderful exercise to help make your aspirations feel more concrete. Once we have declared to ourselves who we want to be, we begin to cultivate more awareness during the times when we are not acting in alignment with this invocation.

Make sure you write your Manifesto down and put it somewhere you will see it every day. The use of strong, affirmative language is also helpful. Own the declaration with statements like: "I exhibit compassion

and sensitivity," or, "I face adversity with strength and clear minded-
ness." Take a few days or weeks to perfect it, recognizing that your manifesto is -- like you - a work in progress.

Meditation: Breath Awareness
This meditation is focused on starting to create a relationship with your
breathing, as the breath is one of the fastest ways to discover what is going on inside. The first step is just to notice how you are breathing right
now. Does your breath feel fast or slow, deep or shallow? Does it feel
smooth or choppy? What are some adjectives you might use to describe
your breath today? After you have taken a minute or two to settle into
awareness of your breath, do this guided meditation to start exploring
your breath a little deeper. Don't forget, the best way to do these meditations is to record them on your phone or computer and then play them
back to yourself because it is much easier to relax if you are being guided
by a voice, especially in the early stages of learning mindful breathing,
instead of trying to memorize the script.

Find a comfortable seat and close your eyes. Take a few moments to
start to relax. Notice your environment: the sounds, smells, and physical sensations that surround you. Let go of judging, or trying to control
the experience, and just imagine you are exploring, holding an attitude
of curiosity in your mind as you see how deeply you can become aware of
this current moment. Continue like this for a little while. Allow yourself to settle in.

Now bring your attention to the breath. Simply notice the breath
as it moves in and out of the body. Allow your awareness to follow the
flow of the breath: in through the nose, down the throat, into the lungs
and belly, then back out from the lungs through the throat and out the
nostrils. See if you can release all control of the breath and pretend the
universe is breathing you. Remember the process of breathing is automatic, so you don't have to do anything to breathe.

Feel how your body responds to the breath. Feel the lungs opening,
the spine lengthening on the in breath, and then the ribs releasing and
the spine surrendering back down to the pull of gravity on the exhale.

Imagine on the in breath you are drawing in positive energy and light and it is expanding through out your body and then on the exhale imagine you are letting go of any tension, toxins, or tightness in the body, releasing it to the universe.

The mind will wander away from the breath. Once you notice you have wandered, just come back into breath awareness. It is that easy. Notice the experiences you have while breathing, allow them to come and go like clouds in the sky. Feel your breath gently move through your body like waves to the shore. Thoughts, emotions, bodily sensations will arise; allow them to move through you, effortlessly like the breath. Just keep returning to awareness of your breath.

I would encourage you to take 5-10 minutes a day to practice this meditation until it becomes a regular part of your life. Before going to sleep is a great place to start. I have been practicing breathing awareness for over 10 years and it has become an invaluable tool to combating stress. I find myself mindfully breathing in my car while in traffic, while doing the dishes, and especially when I am feeling high anxiety while sitting in the dentists' chair. I still catch myself holding my breath at times, or when I am stressed breathing shallowly, but because I have a good mindfulness practice I am much more attuned to noticing the changes in my breath, reacting to the message and reminding myself to slow it down. Breathing helps anchor the present moment and brings forth a sense of space and purpose; it enables me to move through my life with a flow, verses clutching ever so tightly to the things in life that can drive me crazy.

Take Home Message
Cultivating self-awareness allows you to see how your body and thoughts are reacting to your world. This is the first step in reframing your life; it is the inventory process necessary to determine where you are right now. What is the shape and condition of your body? What are your thoughts as you move through your life? What makes you feel better, and what makes you feel worse? You will begin to observe how your mind judges and categorizes things, how it resists certain experiences and tries to

hold onto others. You will build an awareness of your body and posture. You may catch yourself slouching, or notice how confident and strong you feel when you stand upright and tall. This settling down of the mind through awareness allows you to notice your negative tendencies and creates the possibility of letting them go.

Carry this awareness with you into your relationships, your work, and even home to your family. Start weeding out the experiences that do not serve your highest good, letting go of those relationships, beliefs or even physical items that weigh you down. With this awareness you shift from being an unconscious reactor in your life to a conscious creator. You can make the changes you want in order to be the person you want to be. Mindful awareness begins the process of putting you back in the driver's seat of your life. Let's now move a little deeper into the currents of your life and delve into an awareness of your emotions: the navigational system of your life.

3

Emotions: Your Personal Navigational System

"Rather than being your thoughts or emotions be the awareness behind them."

Eckhart Tolle

"Remember, one of the primary reasons we have emotions in the first place is to help us evaluate our experiences."

Jonathan M. Adler

Scott's Story

Scott came to me with complaints of severe anxiety. He noted throughout the day he would be struck by incapacitating periods of a pounding heart, sweaty palms and this driving need to flee immediately, not understanding why. After several sessions it became clear that Scott had a hard time identifying and processing his emotions and the largest emotional trigger in his life was his marriage to Emily.

He described Emily as very sweet and kind 90% of the time, but when she was angry, she would "let loose" on Scott and the kids. As the stories unfolded, it sounded to me that she was verbally abusive towards him and the children, but Scott could not initially see it that way. He repeatedly told me stories of how they were unable to navigate through conflict, for once she started yelling he would become mute and verbally unresponsive which would fuel her anger even more. When I asked him how her behavior made him feel, he stated "I don't know, I never thought about it, I just figured that was how all married couples fought."

As we worked on helping Scott identify his emotions, such as anxiety or anger, he began to identify his feelings within the marriage. He also began to realize how he shut down emotionally when he was feeling strong emotions: it was his protection mechanism. With this new awareness, Scott was able to use the feeling of shutting down as a sign to pay attention, and try to be present and engaged. With practice, he was able to stay emotionally present in arguments and respond back to Emily's tirades. Initially when he began to speak up for himself, Emily became even more verbally aggressive; she was not used to Scott speaking up for himself. Because they were both committed to the relationship working out, they agreed to start marriage counseling.

Through their hard work, both individually and together, Scott and Emily gained a great deal of awareness of their feelings and how their habituated reactions affected each other. Emily could see how her escalating anger pushed Scott to withdraw and Scott could see how his withdrawal left Emily feeling abandoned. They learned how to better manage their emotions, take responsibility for their feelings, and how to ask for what they needed. Scott learned specifically to ask for space when he was feeling overwhelmed or abused. They became able to identify what they were feeling and talk about their emotional needs, rather than digress into past behavioral patterns that attempted to manipulate the other person.

When looking at their family's behavioral patterns, it was not surprising to learn that Scott's wife came from a highly verbal, emotionally reactive family, whereas Scott came from a conflict avoidant family. Emily's family had allowed their emotions to dictate their interactions whereas Scott's family had deemed emotions too dangerous to pursue. It has been a learning process for both of them, but through using mindful awareness, first with their own emotions and consequent behavior patterns, and then with the way they affected one another, they have learned to resolve conflict more effectively. Scott has learned to identify his emotions and stay present with them when expressing himself, and Emily learned to reign in her reactive emotions to give her husband the space to participate. It is not yet perfect, but it is much better, and with greater and greater self-awareness they both will learn to read their emotions as messages that something is going on within themselves and not be so quick to blame the other person.

The Astonishing Power of Emotions

This chapter is all about emotions - those nebulous inner pulls we get as we walk through life. Most people do not even consider their emotional life until they have hit a breaking point and arrive in my office feeling overwhelmed and out of control. I often hear, "I am having a nervous breakdown." This is just code for, "I have not been paying attention to my emotional needs and now they are desperately trying to get my attention." I challenge these clients to consider a reframe of this thought: instead of having a breakdown, perhaps this is a break*through*, as their emotions are trying to tell them something is drastically out of balance.

One of the greatest injustices in life, I believe, is that most of us were not taught to navigate our emotional landscapes. When things in life turn quickly into the realm of unpleasant - we lose a job, experience the death of a loved one, or an unexpected illness in ourselves - we feel a complete loss of control over our lives and the consequent emotional reaction feels overwhelming. We have been taught to push away, push down or just avoid altogether our feelings of pain and discomfort. When these avoidance tactics don't work, some of us collapse into a pit of depression, throwing our arms up in the air in an act of learned helplessness. We tell ourselves a story that supports the idea that our negative emotions are bad and must be avoided at all costs. This is so far from the truth. Our emotions are our own personal navigation system, guiding us into a ever-deepening awareness and acceptance of what it means to be human as well as being guideposts for us, pointing out what is working and what is not, so we may make appropriate changes to create more happiness and contentedness in our lives. Until we are able to befriend all of our emotions, they will control us and our behavior.

Learning to use your emotions as the primary navigational system in life will liberate you from attachment to the ever-changing nature of the physical world and empower you to cultivate a steady state of calm within. As you develop a relationship with your emotions and understand fully that *this too shall pass*, you will be able to surrender the need to control your environment as you become adept at allowing the condition of your internal landscape to be the driving force in your life. Your emotions point to your needs, and your needs point to your happiness. Therefore, learning the language of our emotions is the key to living a happy, healthy life.

What are Emotions?

Emotions are a natural part of our existence. They are the interface where a sensation becomes a feeling which then becomes an experience in our bodies that creates a force in our lives. They give meaning, color and texture to our life experiences. We take chances because we're excited for new prospects, we cry because we've been hurt, and we make sacrifices because we love.

In 1972, psychologist Paul Eckman suggested that there are six basic emotions that are universal throughout human cultures: fear, disgust, anger, surprise, happiness, and sadness. In 1999, he expanded this list to include a number of other basic emotions including embarrassment, excitement, contempt, shame, pride, satisfaction, and amusement. These emotions serve a wide variety of purposes. They help us make decisions, understand ourselves and others, and motivate us to action.

They give us the tools and resources we need to interact meaningfully in our social worlds.

Experiencing emotions is highly subjective as our interpretation of information coming in is filtered through our own past experiences, our current mood and framework through which we see our lives. When we are depressed, everything takes on a dull, gray hue. But when we are riding the high of happiness, joy and love, life is brilliant, and bursting with color. Our emotional life is so powerful it literally dictates how we experience our life. When we are not mindful of our emotions and the power they have over our life experience, we become victims to our reactions and the powerful drives of the limbic system to seek pleasure and avoid pain based on past experiences.

The catch 22 in our emotional life is this: emotions affect our behaviors, define our lives but our behaviors also affect our emotions. If we keep doing things that make us feel good we habituate feelings of well-being and contentedness, but if we continue to do things that make us feel badly, we perpetually experience negative emotions. This is why moment-to-moment awareness of how you are feeling is so important. By tracking your emotional state you can begin to see how you are recreating the experience you have of your emotions again and again and again.

The Effects of Stress and Negative Emotions

As discussed in Chapter 2, our middle brain is instinctively programmed to avoid pain and move towards pleasure. It is in essence the function of the fight, flight or freeze system in our brain. When we are not consciously regulating our emotional state, being mindful of how we feel and how we are reacting, we will default to this system taking control. This is set up to ensure our survival. The middle brain is constantly surveying the environment, looking for patterns of things that might cause us harm or pain, and when it gets a match, an alarm goes off. This alarm may be a twinge of apprehension or it could be a full-fledged panic attack. Whatever it takes to get our attention and motivate us into action. This is what happens with anxiety: usually an innocuous stimulus is perceived as threatening based on a past experience that was painful or dangerous, the recognition pattern launches us into a defensive response.

Unfortunately, these primitive responses are rather two dimensional and not equipped to appropriately interpret our complicated modern culture. In our evolutionary past, we would go through periods of intense stress and then extended periods of rest. This gave our bodies time to metabolize the stress hormones that were released during the times of danger and our physiological system was able to reset. In our modern society, stress doesn't seem to let up. Many people harbor anxiety and worry about daily events and relationships. An unhealthy adaptation of a system that was meant for self preservation, now is ruled by cultural fears such as failure or rejection. Stress hormones continuously wash through our systems in high levels, never leaving the blood and tissues, and we are never able to fully rest and regenerate. And so, the stress response that once gave ancient people the speed and endurance to escape life-threatening dangers runs constantly in our bodies today and never shuts down. This has devastating consequences on our health and happiness. Chronic elevations in stress hormones suppress the immune system, increase the risk of infections and other diseases, and reduce the efficacy of metabolism which leads to obesity. It raises our blood pressure and heart rate, reduces our cognitive abilities, and often results in feelings of exhaustion, disempowerment, chronic anxiety and depression.

Because most of us were not taught to use our emotions as information, we have become victims of our own self-preservation mechanism. I have seen many people spend their entire lives on automatic pilot. They are running from pain in the endless pursuit of pleasure, victims of an instinctive defense mechanism gone awry. The truth is our emotions are the most important ally we have to empower ourselves and reframe our lives. They are a barometer that tells us how we are doing on our path to owning our power and creating a life full of love and peace.

Let's do an experiment. Take a moment to consider the word hate. Close your eyes and let the word float around in your awareness and see what it does to your state of being. Imagine any memories or situations you have experienced that come up when you think of the emotion hate.

Sit with it and just notice how your body, your breath and even your thoughts react to the word. After a few moments, switch to focus on love. Once again take a few minutes to meditate on the word love and see how it affects your state of being. Imagine things you love and drop into the emotional state it solicits. Pay attention to your breathing, your body posture, and your thoughts.

Most people will experience a shift in their emotional state when considering these two oppositional words. A client, Anne, reported she literally felt her heart close when she thought about hate and open when she thought about love. This is a pretty radical reaction, but it demonstrates perfectly how dramatically our bodies are affected by our thoughts and emotions. These reactions are caused by a shift in the biochemistry of your brain. Like a fire burning through a field of dry grasses, your neurons react within milliseconds to what you are focusing on, setting off a powerful cascade of chemical reactions in your brain. Neurons literally light up different areas of your brain associated with patterned reactions to each word — albeit hate or love. These reactions in turn affect your entire body system, causing you to experience an emotion.

When a person is habitually focusing on negative, self defeating thoughts they are literally recreating that physiological state over and over again. People who repeatedly focus on positive thoughts do the same. As a consequence, those who repeatedly think positive thoughts have stronger immune systems, are better able to cope with adversity, feel more content with life, report experiencing more joyful situations, feel loved and supported and manage their stress more effectively. By mindfully watching our attitudes, emotions and stress levels, we actually change the neurochemical transmissions in the body, shifting from an environment of harmful self defeating biochemicals to an environment of uplifting, mood enhancing biochemicals. The power of a healthy attitude therefore cannot be underestimated in the body-mind connection.

The Avoidance of Our Emotional Selves

Often I find clients believe they have no control over their emotions, and live on a perpetual wheel of chasing the good feelings and trying to run away from the bad, blaming the world along the way for every discomfort. They believe if they were to embrace their unpleasant emotions they would be overwhelmed and unable to function. This cannot be further from the truth. Our emotions are information: very important information about the stories we tell ourselves and how we are interpreting information coming in from the outside.

The problems that arise from denying, avoiding, and hiding our feelings can be seen everywhere. External manifestations of this suppression can be seen early on in life. Boys being told at an early age not to cry, who end up punching someone instead; or for girls who are afraid to express their anger and channel their negative feelings into malicious gossip. The internal manifestations of avoiding our emotions might be even more devastating: substance abuse, self neglect and harming behaviors, and ultimately, taking ones life. As adults we can see the consequences of repressed behaviors in the man who's afraid of saying how he feels, and instead buries himself in his work and neglects his family. Or in the woman who can't say "no" because she fears letting people down, yet ends up sexually unresponsive to her husband because she is so divorced from her passion in life.

When we chronically avoid our emotions our energy can become severely depleted. Remember, emotions are energy in motion, so when they are not able to flow fluidly, energy becomes stuck. Buried emotions - the ones we have been running from for years, maybe decades - can create chronic fatigue and depression as well as irritability, anger, insomnia, difficulty with interpersonal relationships, lack of ambition or motivation, lethargy, difficulty accepting yourself, emotional sensitivity and instability as well as a profound feeling of loneliness. Buried emotions affect our physical health by contributing to heart disease, chronic pain and immune disorders.

Perhaps this image will help you understand how harmful ignoring our emotions can be. Imagine a serene stream, gently flowing through the countryside. Every so often someone comes by and throws a large rock (emotional blockage) into the stream. Eventually the flow of the stream becomes clogged as more and more rocks are thrown into the path of the running water. Over the course of a lifetime, the water slowly becomes turbulent, and eventually may become completely blocked. As the pressure builds from the blockage of energy flow, the stream may eventually break through the rocks, creating much damage and flooding.

This is an excellent analogy for what is often perceived as a "breakdown." A breakdown occurs when these suppressed/repressed/denied emotions, which have been held in for so long, eventually break through. The flood of feelings is often so overwhelming they render the person incapable of functioning. The alternative to this may be much worse. If the vital energy of emotions is chronically blocked and never allowed to flow, the energy eventually evolves into matter. Suppressed emotions can become tumorous, hardened arteries, stiff joints, and weakened bones. They can tax the immune system, precipitate the onset of cancer and make a body vulnerable to a number illnesses.

Being disconnected from our emotions also anesthetizes us from feeling empathy towards others: which unleashes the worst of human behavior. When people cut themselves off from their emotional selves they begin to behave from a selfish perspective which may materialize in many guises: oppression, racism, sexism, violence and even war. We cannot intentionally hurt another person -- or animal, plant, or ecosystem - when we are connected to our emotions, because we understand the affect our actions are going to have. When connected we have empathy and understand fully the consequences of our actions. By monitoring our reactions, and mindfully responding to life, we feel at peace with our lives.

With mindful awareness we can turn all of this dysfunction around and gift ourselves with the ability to remain calm and centered in any situation. We begin to use our emotions as tools, and not triggers. Utilizing information from our emotions enables us to pay attention to what is not in alignment in our lives, so we can see where we are not being honest or forthright. With courage and patience we can begin to shine a light on all the dark places we have been trying to hide. This is where we start to get honest about what is and is not working in our lives. Using emotions as a guide, we start to make the changes needed to live the life we want. Let's start to explore the most powerful tool we have to reframe our stories to reframe our lives. Let's learn to reframe our emotions.

The Feedback Loop of Emotions

Emotions are produced through a series of chemical reactions in the brain. They come from the "rush" of happiness that a person feels at getting a good grade on a test, to the "lows" of sadness when someone loses a job. As information about our environment comes in through our nerve impulses and enters our brains, it is coded into a sophisticated system of chemical triggers that create an emotional reaction. The primary "chemical communicators," or neurotransmitters, are the messengers through which all this information is processed. Repetitive exposure to specific thought patterns, say a positive or negative thought, create a habituated emotional reaction. Our subconscious begins to expect a certain response even before all the information becomes known to our conscious mind. This is how emotional responses become habits.

There are an estimated 86 billion cells in the brain called neurons that are responsible for this transfer of information. They communicate various bits of information by secreting chemicals over small gaps between the cells called synapses. When one neuron is charged into action, it releases its chemical messenger, which then moves across the synapse to the next neuron, where it is accepted by a special receiving area, called a receptor. The chemical will be accepted only by receptors that recognize it, in a kind of "lock and key" relationship. Meaning certain keys work only in certain locks. We have hundreds of different receptors on one cell. Once attached to a receptor site on a neuron, a message is transferred; either "go" signals that prompt the neuron to pass certain messages on to other cells or "stop" signals that prevent certain messages from being forwarded.

When thinking about the influence of thoughts on the brain, remember this: our brains are always looking for a shortcut to processing information, as there is too much information coming in to be processed at once. As a consequence, brain cells are constantly being grouped or

LARA KAIN PA-C, MPAS

"wired" into associative relationships, hence the expression, "neurons that fire together wire together." It is kind of like the spectator wave in a sports stadium: once a certain group of cells are activated, there is a chain reaction that perpetuates a habituated response. In the stadium analogy, at first there are only a few fans that stand up, but as time passes, the energy gains momentum and the wave grows larger and larger. Eventually there is a visual experience of a wave moving through the stadium. And each time the fans are encouraged to wave, the response time is faster and faster. When brain cells communicate frequently, the connection between them strengthens -- just like the wave - and with enough repetitions the reaction becomes a habit.

Messages that travel along the same pathway in the brain over and over begin to transmit faster and faster. This is why it takes effort to overcome a habit, you have to convince your brain that what it once thought was good now needs to be disbanded and a new set of associations needs to be created in its place. Since the brain is always looking for ways to save energy, this is not a very appealing proposition. And so it takes practice to create new neural pathways. Have you ever tried to learn to play an instrument? You know how hard it is to overcome that initial hump of complete disorganization, your fingers just have no idea what they are doing. If you stick with it, eventually it becomes easier and easier as your brain creates more and more connections that become habituated.

This habituation happens with our stories as well. Let's say you perpetually feel strong emotional responses to your boss and you label this emotion as "feeling victimized." Your brain cells will create a pathway associated with a past experience of victimization, let's say you had an overbearing father. So every time your boss does something that feels remotely threatening, like your overbearing father, your brain cells light up and have a party and tell you you are being victimized. Your brain will create a story to reinforce this feeling being true, even when it is only true in your head. To a great degree this is how our brains create the world we see. We are wired to assume and react.

When our brains sees any type of pattern that supports a particular story the neurons fire up, piecing together a familiar narrative. If we are depressed we will see life through this lens of depression: our brains will light up in a neurochemical party anytime we see something that feels depressing such as a cloudy sky, a bill, a lonely man at the bus stop. On the other hand, someone who is not depressed may interpret these same things in a completely different way: a cloudy sky means water for their garden; when paying the bills they feel gratitude for being able to afford luxuries in life; and the solitary man at the bus stop is not lonely, but perhaps just lost in contemplation. We rarely question our assumptions, and feel confident we know what is really going on out there in the real world, but do we? Most often we do not, we are living in our own created stories of what life is. That is why we get into so much trouble making assumptions; remember the catch phrase, assuming makes and ASS out of U and ME.

It might sound incredible to imagine that by intentionally focusing attention on the moment-to-moment experiences, without being swept up in judgments or expectations, we can actually change the structural connections in our brain. Focusing on positive events and circumstances and imagining best case scenarios, literally rewires the brain away from negative patterns into utilizing positive ones. The term is called neuroplasticity and reflects the brain's ability to grow and change based on the challenges life presents and how we perceive them. Present centered awareness, as reviewed in chapter 2, enhances neuroplasticity as it allows us to get out of our emotional center and into a rational, calm, problem-oriented space to create change. When we hit a speed bump, either literally or figuratively, and give ourselves the time to stop and and drop into what is really going on, we learn to stop collapsing into our automatic reactions and step back and just observe what is going on. By practicing with this simple, yet powerful tool, we allow our brain the freedom to be open and curious, rather than being fearful and apprehensive.

The more you practice being aware of the present moment through your breath, you will start to learn how to keep your body calm when you feel an emotion and resist shifting automatically into an unconscious assumption and reaction. When we intervene with awareness, learn to

LARA KAIN PA-C, MPAS

perceive, feel and act differently, this shifts the chemical response and electrical wiring in our brains. We literally rewire our brains each time we reframe our thoughts.

The Visceral Reaction of Emotions

As our brains are experiencing a perpetual rush of chemical tides, our bodies respond to these chemicals via bodily sensations. The trick is to start to understand that the physiological reactions we have, are just that: reactions, without any inherent meaning. A pounding heart, tingling skin and sweaty palms could mean multiple things. Even if the emotion is anxiety, it could be the rush of norepinephrine which prompts us to action, perhaps to run across a street when we see a car heading straight for us or the anticipatory anxiety we may experience before giving a big presentation to our peers, which helps us to stay focused and on point. Where we get stuck is when we become hyper-focused on the bodily reactions and lose sight of the fact that these sensations are just information. If we can stay present in the moment, the feeling will pass soon enough. It is when we try to resist an emotion that we start giving energy to a story and lose touch with what is really going on, thus perpetuating the negative emotion.

It is our resistance to the experience and hyper-focusing on sensations we don't like that perpetuate the cycle of negative emotions and rewires our brains. Your body responds to the way you think, feel, and act. An interesting example of this is found within the halls of medical schools. Up to 75% of medical students report developing symptoms suggestive of the illnesses they are studying. Because they are engrossed in pathology, how things can go wrong in the body, they get hyper-focused on bodily reactions and misinterpret them, thinking they are sick. Luckily for the students, the curriculum quickly moves on to the next illness or disease process, and the symptoms are easily forgotten. But there are people who spend days, to weeks, to months, to years worrying or resisting a sensation which will eventually manifest that which is being resisted: a disease, a job loss, financial failure, whatever fear the mind can manifest.

A wonderful way to see this in 3D is to look at the results of a study done in Finland that mapped heat flow through human bodies as people were experiencing different emotions. Participants were asked to map out where they felt different emotions on their bodies. The results were astounding. People reported that happiness and love sparked activity across nearly the entire body, while depression had the opposite effect; it dampened feelings in the arms, legs and head. Danger and fear triggered strong sensations in the chest area, and anger was one of the few emotions that activated the arms. Interesting that when we feel angry we have the urge to hit or throw something. It beautifully illustrates the multidimensional nature of our emotions. This study was published in the Proceedings of the National Academy of Sciences, by Lauri Nummennaa at al. Look it up, it is fascinating.

The Messages of Our Emotions

Now that you have a good understanding of what emotions are and how they affect our bodies, the next step is to understand what information each emotion is communicating. We are quite good at knowing why we have pleasant emotions, the swell of love we feel for our children or the pride we feel after achieving a hard-earned goal. I would like to focus more on the unpleasant emotions most try to avoid. Our culture tends to shame, silence, devalue, and deny negative feelings. We are frequently told to "get past," or "get over it." We learn to control, manage, and medicate these unruly, destructive forces. But control and get over we cannot. The more we turn our backs on our emotions, the more they bubble over into all kinds of unhealthy behaviors. When we are able, instead, to accept our unpleasant emotions with mindful awareness and recognize there is a message imbued in them, we can start to better understand ourselves and reframe our story.

Emotions have become polarized in our culture: they are seen as either good or bad. Thus, love, excitement and joy are seen as *good* emotions, whereas anxiety, sadness and anger are seen as *bad* emotions. We struggle with highly distressing emotions, such as extreme anger, or sadness and can even feel guilty or ashamed when we try to discuss what we are struggling with in our lives. Such reactions undoubtedly stem from our culture's overriding bias toward positive thinking. Although positive emotions are worth cultivating, and contribute greatly to a healthy life, problems arise when people start believing they must be upbeat all the time. Unpleasant feelings are just as crucial as the enjoyable ones in helping make sense of life's ups and downs.

The process of resisting or rejecting unwanted emotions is a rejection of self and cuts us off from a sense of meaning, growth and understanding when confronting life's adversities. The act of resisting the emotion actually back fires in the end as it brings what we are wanting to avoid front and center in our mind. The more you resist, deny, try to avoid, the more it will keep popping up in your life. In a 2009 study, psychologist David J. Kavanagh of Queensland University of Technology in Australia asked people in treatment for alcohol abuse and addiction to complete a questionnaire that assessed their drinking-related urges and cravings, as well as any attempts to suppress thoughts related to alcohol in a 24 hour period. The study found that those who often fought against intrusive alcohol-related thoughts actually harbored more of them, making it harder to resist the urges.

I find in my own practice, client's come in feeling depressed and then report feeling guilty for being depressed. They invalidate their own experiences with statements like, "Why should I feel depressed when I have my health, a good job, I am secure financially and my kids are doing well?" By judging depression as "bad" the associative feelings of guilt which result only perpetuate more feelings of depression and disempowerment. Because not only does the person feel depressed, but in their inability to accept their current emotional state, they are feeling guilty too.

Negative emotions offer us an opportunity to slow down and consider what the message is that our inner self is sending. The reason we call them negative is that they don't make us feel good and are generally perceived in our body by an uncomfortable sensation, like a clenched heart or upset stomach. We could turn this story around and look for the gift in each negative feeling. Fear becomes an emotional alarm system that alerts us to pay attention and to act in the interest of life and survival. It reminds us of our human frailty, and teaches us humility. When we are able to feel our fear and move ahead in spite of it, we are able to know courage and strength in adversity. *Anger* is generally born out of a feeling of an injustice, whether towards ourselves or others, and generally points to unmet needs or desires. *Guilt* helps us to see who we are and who we want to be. *Intense guilt* causes us to evaluate our behaviors and determine whether they are in alignment with our beliefs. *Sadness* brings forward our vulnerability in this world and gives us an opportunity to ask for help. It connects us to empathy and compassion for the human condition, for when we are mindfully aware we realize everyone suffers. And lastly, despair is the source of a hunger for meaning, it is what drives us to grow and expand. Each of these emotional states offer an opportunity to grow out of an old way of seeing the world and reframe into a new vision of life.

Our emotions give voice to our deepest inner needs. The pain we feel is a call to awaken to the fact that we are doing something that is not in alignment with our desires. Painful emotions need not constrict, isolate, or devastate us. They can open and expand us, bring attention to what needs to be addressed and strengthen our empathic connections to others and to the world. They are not telling you how to behave - the habits you have developed in response to them are doing that. Emotions do not give permission to yell, isolate or get depressed. They are acting as messengers to motivate you to ask for what you need, to have the courage to defend your boundaries, change a situation that is abusive or to choose to walk away from whatever might be hurting you. If we are able to heed the call of our negative emotions -- practice sitting with the discomfort and recognizing this pain is just a call to change -- we can begin to move through these periods of discomfort with the hope and knowledge that this is a message from our own inner wisdom and if we heed the call with awareness and integrity, it will lead the way to growth and empowerment.

Befriending Our Emotions
I hope by this time you can see how important it is to learn to flow with your emotions rather than try to deny, control or resist them. One of

the easiest ways to befriend your emotions is to use mindful awareness when you are experiencing them. From the first push or pull we feel in response to something, to the throes of a complete emotional meltdown, we always have the opportunity to stop, breathe and observe. The first step is to check in and assess what we are feeling. So often we feel something moving within us but are unable to label what the emotion is. Two UCLA studies showed "that simply labeling emotion promotes detachment," says David Creswell, Ph.D., a meditation researcher at the university who joined colleague Matthew D. Lieberman, Ph.D., in heading up the research. As you learn to open up to your emotions with awareness and non-judgement, what you may experience as anger might actually be disappointment. Perhaps the anxiety you experience is really fear of judgement. Take some time to develop a deeper level of self-awareness so you can accurately describe your emotional experience.

The other side of emotional mastery is learning to express your emotions. It is an important part of healthy and mature communication. Consider the following statements:

"You made me angry" versus "I feel angry."

Do you notice any differences in the feelings they solicit?

There is a subtle but powerful shift in emphasis between the two. The former places blame and assumes that the other person is responsible. The second statement effectively communicates the same feeling but eliminates blame and indicates a personal acknowledgment and acceptance of the internal experience. In communicating with another human being, the second statement is more of a report rather than an accusation. I've found taking the blame out of our emotions to be a powerful tool for learning how to communicate in a more mature and healthy way. This is a tool I teach my clients how to use early on to help them understand they are responsible for their feelings and the only way to be able to utilize the information is for them to take ownership.

When we have the courage to let our emotions flow, something unexpected, unpredictable, even miraculous, happens: we allow a space for healing to occur within ourselves and in our relationships. Where once there was a hole in our heart, we now experience *wholeness*. Where we felt paralysis from fear, we experience *courage* and *trust*. From the apparent stasis of despair, something shifts and motivates us to *ask for more from our lives*. Unimpeded and mindfully experienced, the energy of the emotions are opportunities to flow *toward healing and harmony*.

Here is an exercise that will help you befriend your emotions and start learning to use your story to change your feelings. Carry a journal around with you for the next week. Make notes at hourly intervals on your primary feelings. First observe whether you are feeling positive or negative. Then see if you can further describe your emotions. Are you angry? Tired? Stressed? Happy? Excited? Cheerful? Exhausted? Delirious? Write them all down, and then jot down some notes about what is going on inside and outside of you at this time. If you have a hard time beginning to name your emotions get a mood chart, there are many free versions online that can assist you in identifying what you are really feeling.

Eventually you will develop a new vernacular for your feelings and be able to better articulate how circumstances affect you. Learning this new skill brings forth an opportunity to understand ourselves better and be more accepting of our internal states. Again, the point is not to assign judgment or to determine why you are feeling a particular emotion. Questioning "why" starts the story telling process. It gives an opportunity to side step owning the emotions through the process of pointing blame and creating rationalizations. You are merely observing and identifying feelings to garner greater self-awareness.

Another helpful exercise is to find ways to shift the energy with things you love. Using music and art are two easy ways to alter your emotional state. I have a play list on my phone called "Change Your State." When I start to feel negativity pulling me down I play it for a few minutes and more often than not I find myself happy, dancing and ready to embrace the rest of my day. Listening to uplifting Youtube videos or calling a friend are easy ways to shift your state as well as playing with a child or a pet. Find memories, thoughts, or people you love to think about. Journal about times in your life that you really enjoyed yourself or the pride you felt by accomplishing something really hard. Doodling, coloring mandalas or working on a collage are excellent art projects that can move you into a better frame of reference. Create your own list of emotional transformers and have them ready to pull out when you feel those first tugs of a negative mood state.

The Gift

There are no 'positive' or 'negative' emotions; there is only information. What we experience as emotions are neurological programs which have evolved over our lifetimes to help us make the best choices we can to survive and ultimately improve our lives. By being mindful of our emotional reactions we begin to understand the nuances and messages our emotions are trying to tell us about ourselves and our environments. This awareness helps us to identify when emotions are coming up. We can learn to channel this information into appropriate action rather than allowing it to trigger a habituated response. Negative emotions are a stronger call to assess what is going on internally and externally, to ask better questions, and then actively utilize the wisdom imbued in our emotions to consciously act in accordance with our desired path. When we can relate to our emotions with curiosity and authenticity, we can access our innermost wisdom and begin to see who we really are without stories to cloud our vision.

The content of the stories you tell directly affect your experience. If you are living in fear of your emotions and constantly running from pain, your life will feel empty, lonely and disempowered. If you are able to be open and embrace the full spectrum of the human experience, your life will feel full, exciting and brimming with passion. You may have a bad day here or there, but you will be able to understand this is just a speed bump trying to get your attention. All we need to do is reframe the way we tell our stories about how we feel. Next time you are having a down day, rather than bemoaning all the reasons you may be feeling down, stop, breathe, and ask yourself what message your life may be trying to send you with this blip in your feeling good state. You may be surprised where the answers will take you.

Journal: A Prompt To Name Your Emotions

A great journaling exercise to get familiar with your emotions is to start with the prompt "I feel ...". Set a timer for 2 minutes and just write whatever comes to mind. As with most journaling exercises, please keep writing, even if you go off on a tangent. The more we are able to stop thinking about what we want to say and allow the unconscious mind free reign over the exercise the more effectively we will be at getting to the heart of the emotion. So just write, and don't edit what comes out. Use this technique to explore a wide variety of emotions, such as sadness, fearfulness, loneliness as well as the positive emotions of joy, gratitude and peace. Do this exercise at your own pace, perhaps that will be one emotion a day so you can really sit with each one separately. If you are struggling with naming emotions, look up The Feelings Wheel by Dr. Gloria Willcox. It is a very useful tool to explore your emotions.

Meditation: Sitting with Difficult Emotions

Find a comfortable sitting position and begin with breath awareness. Sit with your breath for a few minutes, and in your mind's eye watch it move in and out of your body. Once you feel settled, bring your awareness to a difficult situation in your life. It may be thoughts of an event in the past that was painful or distressing, it may be something in your life right now that is causing you painful feelings such as difficulty with your partner or boss, or it may be something you are worried about in the future. Allow your attention to focus on one of these worrying thoughts, bringing to mind all the details you can imagine of the uncomfortable situation: where you are; who you are with; the time of day; sights; smells; and what you might be hearing.

Notice how your body responds to this image. Are there places of tension or tightness in your body? What is happening to your breathing? Has it changed from when you started? Don't try to modify the sensations in your body, just notice them with curiosity. Notice any emotions you may be feeling - they may be feelings like sadness, hurt, anger, loneliness, fear or pain. Explore these feelings without getting attached. If you do get stuck, let go of the image and allow your attention to turn back to the breath for a few cycles, bringing you back to your body and the present moment. This is the practice: exploring; getting caught in the distraction; and returning to the breath and the present moment; then moving back into exploring the experience. With practice we create the skill of being with our emotions and not judging or resisting them. When I am having a really hard time letting go of my attachment to an emotion I will imagine myself holding on as a warrior and then invite myself to let go as I see my image shift into that of a monk. With this reframe in images I can feel the need to shift as I envelop an energy of acceptance.

Check in with your thoughts. Are they calm and smooth, or do they become jumpy and choppy, darting all around the landscape of your mind? Remember, thoughts are not facts, they are simply what your mind is creating at any given moment. They may be based in factual events, or they are simply the mind wandering. Consider the thoughts you are having, remember you do not have to react to them, as they are not real. Notice them as they change and when a new thought replaces the previous one.

Start to imagine breathing in fresh air and energy into your body and the situation. Can your body release any tension you may be holding onto? If your heart is clenching, can you begin to soften your heart space? Can you release your belly, soften your facial muscles, and gently reframe your thoughts? Play with the experience and find the areas of tension you can shift as you breathe. When you feel like you have shifted enough, let go of the situations and come back into your breath. Breathing in and breathing out, bringing awareness back into your hands and feet. And when you are ready open your eyes.

A Direct Line to Your Inner Wisdom

Our emotions are powerful indicators to us about what is going on internally, but because many of us either do not know what exactly it is that we are feeling or do not feel safe expressing our feelings, they often are repressed or ignored. This alienates us from the wisdom our emotions inherently offer, as our emotions connect us to the deepest parts of ourselves. They are like beacons in the night of the soul, helping us to see where we need light and love and acceptance. When we can learn to open ourselves up to the full range of emotions without judgement, show courage in the face of fear, vulnerability in grief, compassion in pain, we learn to gracefully endure the lessons life has to give. With this feeling of self-reliance and trust we learn we can handle anything life has to offer, we can begin to tell better stories about ourselves and our lives. We begin to trust the process and know, regardless of what shows up in our lives, we are okay, capable of navigating anything and moving forward.

Now we will move from the internal environment to the outside influences that affect the stories we tell. We will move into the area of all those things that get under our skin and drive us mad and what those irritants have to tell us about ourselves and our stories.

4

Triggers: The Gift Within the Rub

"Our parents, our children, our spouses and our friends will continue to press every button we have, until we realize what it is that we don't want to know about ourselves yet. They will point us to freedom every time."

Byron Katie

"Everything that irritates us about others can lead us to an understanding of ourselves."

Carl Jung

The Smoothie From Hell

$\mathcal{I}$ have been seeing my client Roxanne for many years, and every time her sister-in-law is in town, I would hear about it. Roxanne often felt belittled by her sister-in-law, and her controlling behavior. I was astounded at the level of disrespect my client would endure when her husband's sister came for a visit. At one point, after my client had described her sister-in-law's habit of taking over while she was making a smoothie for her husband, I invited Roxanne to reframe how she saw this situation. Instead of collapsing it into a story of being controlled, and feeling resentful, I asked her to consider not taking it personally but to be curious about the motives behind Denna's behavior. We discussed multiple ways she could address the issue. We decided that the next time she interfered with the smoothie making process that Roxanne would ask an investigative question like, "I'm curious Denna, do you feel I am not capable of making a smoothie?"

As Roxanne was retelling the story, she explained how when she was able to shift her judgment into curiosity, she stopped feeling resentful and controlled. As Denna was poised to take over the blender, Roxanne asked the rehearsed question. Her sister-in-law stared at her for a second or two and then walked out of the kitchen without a word. She has never tried to take control over from Roxanne again. This was a beautiful example of a reframe. It can be as easy as shifting the story from the harshness of conflict to the gentle flow of curiosity. It requires taking a step back, utilizing your breathe to create space for something new, and then not making it personal. Just get curious. And even though my client never got a verbal response, the behavioral response was all she needed.

Soft Overcomes Hard

"Soft overcomes hard" is a quote from the Chinese philosopher Lao Tzu. It explains the process of moving consciously with energy flow rather than fighting against it. The idea goes something like this. When we are confronted with a negative energy/comment/situation and respond in kind, the energy surrounding the situation becomes escalated because both energies are pushing against each other. If instead, when we are confronted with negative energy, we take a step back and try to understand the circumstances from which this energy might have arisen, the energy begins to dissipate.

For example, if someone were to say something unkind to you and you shoot back with something similar, both parties walk away feeling hurt. The energy from the first person grew secondary to the addition of unkind energy from the second person leaving no one feeling good. A softened response would be not to bristle at the comment but rather be curious and inquire about the reason for the comment. This reduces the energy around the interaction and allows room for understanding to ensue. The other person may explain they were having a bad day or were irritated with something you had said earlier. This offers an opportunity for resolution where both parties feel they understand rather than feel hurt. When someone pushes against us, most of us have been taught to reflexively push back with a similar energy. This chapter is about starting to look at emotional discomfort differently, and incorporating a "soft overcomes hard" approach to your emotional life.

We apply this concept of soft overcoming hard in our lives by relaxing our judgements, actively releasing mental anguish and learning to accept the current situation. This means releasing both external and internal judgements. When we push back on external events, people or situations, we shut down any opportunity for growth or resolution; our push back keeps us hard and locked into our own self-righteous judgement. When we push back on ourselves with internal judgements we set ourselves up for self-rejection. For example, the thought, "I am fat" generally is followed by further judgements about why we believe we are fat. This dialogue is actively pushing against what is real, which is futile. If you do realistically weigh too much, a more productive approach would be to admit you are unhappy with the current state of your physical body then use your energy to come up with a plan to change your weight. One of the fastest ways to change your life is to stop wasting your energy running on a hamster wheel of judgment - that only creates more judgment and perpetuates a story of feeling powerless to change your circumstances. These internal negative judgements are only a form of self abuse, they serve no purpose but to punish the offender: YOU.

I would ask you to consider how much time you spend in your head running on that hamster wheel of judgment, allowing the stories to get bigger and bigger? In this state of constantly pointing a finger at a problem a resolution will never be found. The more you push back on yourself and others, the bigger the problems become. So in this chapter we will look at all the things we push back on in our lives: the places where we get hard, and push back, creating more pain for ourselves and others.

Triggers-A Chance at Self Discovery

Up to this point we have been exploring how to calm the inner seas. With a good understanding of these skills, we now turn to where our internal life intersects with the external world. Life is going on outside of us and our participation is mandatory. This juncture of internal meets external is where our greatest growth potential exists. I'm not talking about the good times though, those are the gifts. I'm talking about the hard, challenging times that offer an opportunity to rise above, to discover new strengths and gain greater self confidence. Unfortunately, most of us have been taught to avoid life's challenges and work hard to play it safe. In truth, this is the rub: the place where things outside of us create a negative experience inside of us. This is where we are offered a spring board into personal growth and self mastery if we can learn to reframe our stories.

Ann is an excellent example of how exploring emotional triggers can enhance self awareness. She came to me because she was struggling in her relationship with her daughter, Michelle, since she had left for college. Ann noted she would get painfully triggered when she called her daughter and Michelle would take days to return her phone calls. Ann found that she would be irritable with her daughter when they eventually did talk and she would become very demanding. She noted her irritability and anger would spill onto her relationship with her husband as well, as she would become increasingly irritable with him the more days that passed between calls.

Until Ann began working with me, she did not realize that "unavailability" was a trigger for her. When her daughter did not immediately return her calls, Ann felt vulnerable because she really wanted to talk to her daughter and she felt her daughter did not feel the same. Ann started telling a story about how she must not be very important to her daughter since she did not call back right away. Growing up as the youngest in a family of seven children, Ann began to see how her needs for attention were not met in her childhood, and she was projecting those needs onto her daughter. Now she is learning to be compassionate with her needs and we are working to figure out how she can find a balance between getting her own needs met while maintaining healthy boundaries in her relationship with her daughter.

Instead of avoiding the rubs in life, a healthier reframe is to see the discomfort as a challenge. It's an opportunity to expand our mindset to include new possibilities and creative solutions as well as healing old wounds. Challenges in life strengthen our will, and if faced head on, with an attitude of openness, teach us new tools and life skills. Everything changes when we are able to embrace pain and suffering and see these places where we feel the rub as invitations to look within. With self awareness and the right mental attitude we can completely reframe the way we experience every challenge in life and with practice we can come to view these challenges as some of our most valuable life experiences. Wouldn't that be a welcome reframe?

As humans, it is natural to respond emotionally to what is going on around us. When we see a baby smile we feel happy; when a loved one is sick, we feel compassion. The difficulty is when what we see elicits a strong negative emotion. This is where we delve into the world of emotional triggers. A trigger is an element in your environment that causes a strong emotional reaction in you that is disproportionate to the situation itself. To put it another way, when we are triggered we lose touch with our mature, adult, rational brain and instead regress back to places we are emotionally stuck - or as I like to call this: the tar pit of an unhealed emotional wound.

When considering the things we push back on - the places in life where we respond with hard verses soft -- these automatic strong responses come from an old wound that has been reactivated. When you're triggered, you're no longer responding to the present situation. Instead, you're running old software, unwittingly trying to repair or avoid a story that caused pain in the past. Instead of embracing the pain and bringing it into the light, we try to hide it deep within our core and react disproportionately when something comes close to exposing our vulnerability.

Remember in Chapter 3 when we discussed how our brains create powerful chemical associations between things? And the stronger the emotional reaction, the stronger the connections? This is why things that have hurt in the past and have not been healed are so powerful. These unhealed wounds are like a spring-loaded button, and when they are triggered they release a perfect storm of reactive chemicals. When we see a pattern that we recognize, the brain pulls and releases a myriad of chemicals that create a familiar response. A great analogy for this would be if you were struck by lightening. Once you've been hit by lightening, even though you know the odds of it happening again are almost impossible, the sight of a rain cloud will send your pulse racing. If you have not worked through your fear of lightening and come to an understanding that rain clouds do not equate to the pain of a lightening strike, you will perpetually be on guard for the next sign of rain.

You can substitute getting struck by lightening with being abandoned, being physically or sexually abused, growing up with a parent who has a substance abuse problem, growing up poor, neglected or just plain misunderstood. All these painful situations set the stage for feeling triggered when anything in your environment mirrors these wounds. This is what I really want you to learn from this chapter: *most of us are being triggered by responding to old stories from when we were children. Because many of us have not healed the wounds of the past, we have not realized that as mature adults we have complete power over how we are responding to what is happening in our lives right now.*

When we become mindful warriors of inner peace, we learn to use our emotional triggers as a call to pay attention. Like the kick we got from our mothers' under the table when we started to act up as a child, emotional triggers are our warning flags that some old wound is being activated and the brain is mobilizing into a habituated response to make it stop. Most of the pain and discomfort we feel in our lives comes from resisting the messages in these triggers; we allow ourselves to go on automatic pilot, to avoid feeling pain instead of addressing the wounds with mindful awareness. In essence we relinquish control of our lives to our past.

We all have our triggers. Maybe someone made a benign joke about you that sent you over the edge. Or someone asks you to do something and you immediately feel overwhelmed. Or a friend doesn't invite you somewhere and you start to obsessively think that no one likes you. They permeate our lives and, yet, often we are not even aware of them. Something just happens and the next thing we know we find ourselves in emotional turmoil.

The reframe for these triggers involves putting on your curious glasses. Rarely do we think to ask ourselves what these triggers might be saying about us. Each time we feel the pull of irritation, anger or anxiety, we could get curious and ask how might this feeling give us insight into ourselves and the wounds that are negatively influencing our lives? This chapter is going to explore just this question: how is our outside world mirroring what needs to be addressed on the inside? Where in the rub of your life might there be an opportunity to heal, grow and expand your understanding of yourself and others? How might you be able to embrace the philosophy of soft overcoming hard to create a more balanced, peaceful life?

So we move from awareness of self and our emotions into the territory of our environment to see how what is happening *out there* can help us understand what is going on *in here*. We will explore our triggers and start to discern the gift within the rub. We will learn to tease out what our triggers might be, and then with mindfulness, slow down our tendency to react so we may have space to inquire about what exactly inside of us is asking to be healed.

Emotional Pain: A Request for Self Compassion

Try this experiment. Close your eyes and think of someone who repeatedly gets under your skin. It can be a sibling, neighbor, co-worker or maybe even your spouse. Bring them into mind and the issues you have with them. Notice how you feel. What emotions come up for you? How does your breathing or body posture change? What thoughts and judgements arise when you think about this person? What is the theme of the story you have been telling about this person who triggers you? Are they too loud, too insensitive, too dumb, too immature, too fat? Take some time to consider the story you are telling yourself about this person. When you feel you have a good handle on your story, I want you to reframe the image and imagine you are someone who loves this person, or a time when you felt love for this person. Perhaps imagine their spouse, or parents showering them with unconditional love. As the perspective shifts, does your story change? Can you imagine their suffering, what they might experience when you judge them? What is pushing back within you when this person comes into your life? What need or desire do you have that is not being met in your relationship with this person and what could you do to change it? The next time you interact with this person after doing this exercise, notice if your story changes. See if you can try to be a little softer in your reaction and ask what your judgement is revealing about you.

The key is to recognize the triggers in your life so you can become more intentional in how you respond. It is vitally important to explore the source of our triggers so we can start to reframe the present with empowering stories rather than disempowering reactions. With the skill of mindful awareness and the ability to stay in control when we are triggered, we can catch ourselves in our stories, take a deep breath and offer compassion to ourselves and others as we choose an action towards healing instead of a reaction to guard against pain.

I would encourage you to consider your triggers as reminders to take a step back in your life and get curious about what is coming up for you. During times of emotional upset, if we can have compassion for our pain, our emotional reactions begin to soften. If we can take a step back and listen to our inner voice as well as the people and situations that are triggering us, we will be able to see things from a less reactive position and be better able to understand why we get so upset. To help you start to identify the triggers in your life, we will explore three common ones: buttons, potholes and rascals.

Buttons, Potholes and Rascals, Oh My!

The first of the three main triggers I work with are buttons. Buttons are the subtle mannerisms, attitudes or behaviors exhibited in others, that push us into a frenzy. If you have ever been married you know what I am talking about. It is amazing how adept our spouses become at pushing our buttons. There is also, always, the stranger who cuts in line at the grocery store, or when a family member leaves dishes in the sink, not rinsed. Buttons trigger an automatic negative emotional response: usually a habituated unconscious judgement which is enshrouded in anger and indignation. Buttons are the icing on a bad day cake. The interesting thing about buttons is that their intensity fluctuates depending on your current emotional state. Ever notice how you are more triggered when you are having a bad day, and that you are better able to let things slide when you are having a good one?

Our emotional buttons are closely related to our needs. We all need to feel loved and accepted by others. These are healthy, normal human needs. Buttons come to be triggered when we have not learned to ask for what we need and yet expect others to know what we want. If unmet needs become very strong and intense, they begin to take over our lives. Your buttons could be costing you a lot. You may be righteously angry, but negative emotional reactions to unmet needs rob you of power and reinforce the story that things outside of you need to be a certain way in order for you to be happy.

Our buttons are our soft spots, the places where we have not healed our inner wounds. And so when they get triggered they are asking for you to take a look inside at what needs are not being met. Anger and indignation will never make you happy in the long run. The reframe here is to stop blaming external circumstances and people for your unmet needs. When you get angry, recognize it's your anger and yours to explore. When we allow ourselves to give into the emotional reactiveness of our buttons, we are surrendering our power to external situations. Something happens and we react. Remember, only you can give situations permission to control you based on your reactions, and the stories you tell. Once you are able to identify your buttons and understand where they are coming from, then you can start to tease out their emotional pull, and consciously center yourself to create a plan to get your needs met.

Emotional potholes are those life situations that we know are coming, and we know are going to be uncomfortable, and yet refuse to confront. You know what I am talking about. It's those situations you can see coming from miles away, or months ahead of time, and yet, you fall in every time. A perfect example is the dreaded Thanksgiving dinner with extended family where you are too afraid to hurt people's feelings to say you aren't coming. Every year you try a different coping mechanism to make it through unscathed: perhaps mindful breathing one year, Valium the next, and yet you fall into the same pattern of leaving the gathering feeling badly and fantasizing about standing up for yourself next year. But you never do and these dinners continue to recur and cause great discomfort.

How is it that over the course of so many years, we still get triggered? I mean, we know the in-laws are coming, we know our spouse loves to spend money on gifts and we know the neighbors are storing those life sized Christmas elves with glee in the garage, just waiting until Thanksgiving to start busting them out. So why do we allow these things to continuously annoy us year after year, robbing us of our inner peace?

These are our emotional potholes. Situations we have convinced ourselves we have no power to change and therefore feel overwhelmed by feelings of victimization. Have you heard the quote "insanity is doing the same thing over and over again and expecting a different result?" This is where we find ourselves with our potholes. One of the largest ways we disempower ourselves with our stories is continuing to do the same thing over and over again and expecting the situation to change. If you want your world to change, change yourself.

Emotional potholes offer us an opportunity to make adjustments within ourselves and our situations to create a more fulfilling experience. My client, Mary, came up with a great pothole reframe. She had an uncle who hijacked family holidays with stories of the past. He would talk over other family members, dominating the conversation until he had everyone's attention and stole the show. The problem was they were the same stories, year after year, and this behavior really put a damper on the holiday cheer as everyone was trying to figure out how to control Uncle Bob. Mary's solution was to start a tradition of game playing after the family meal. This reframe was a great success. Everyone in the family now looks forward to the holidays and Mary feels her reframe has greatly improved communication skills within the family and created a more intimate holiday experience. I invite you to consider the situations you dread in your life, and start to get curious about how you could reframe your thoughts about them to problem solve your way to a better experience.

When reframing your emotional potholes, please remember this: events and situations do not have inherent meaning, we determine how we are going to interpret a given event. Before you start collapsing into the normal negative rhetoric you experience when anticipating an uncomfortable event, stop yourself, center, and then actively look for positive ways to reframe the situation. Even if it means just acknowledging the situation is going to be uncomfortable and possibly painful, and that you are choosing to engage in it because you want to. Just by reframing something into a choice you are shifting a lot of negative victim energy. So the next time you feel the dread of an upcoming event, take it as sign to reframe your thoughts into something you are looking forward to experiencing, even if it is the relief you will feel when the event is over.

Most of us spend a large part of our lives trying to control the little rascals that drive us crazy. From our children and pets, to our spouse or strangers on the street. They are the people in our lives that just get under our skin at one time or another and we feel it is our duty to change them. In essence what we are trying to do is control other people so we may feel better, and when that does not work, we blame them for making us unhappy. Here is the irony of trying to control another person: when you try to control someone else's behavior, ultimately they are controlling you. You are acting in response to *their* actions, not on your own accord. The truth is the only person we can control is ourselves. The reframe here comes from letting go of your story about them and trusting that your irritation is pointing out something that needs to change within you, and not the other person.

When I first present this theory of rascals to clients I often get push back. They will argue that they are not the angry, violent, depressed, guilt-ridden, critical, or complaining person that this supposed "mirror/teacher" is reflecting. The problem lies with the other person, right? Wrong. It would be convenient if we could always place the blame on the other person, but this is not always so easy.

Every person you meet has a message to give you about yourself if you are open to receiving it. Each encounter, whether good or bad, offers the gift of greater self awareness by illustrating what you do and do not accept about yourself. Those rascals in your life are just putting an exclamation point behind all the things you are trying to hide about yourself. When you practice the art of reframing, you start to see that the judgements you make about every person you meet is just a reflection of how you see yourself.

With mindful awareness you can begin to see how what you judge in others is actually tied to some judgement you have about yourself. Some common examples of this are the unfaithful husband who suspects his wife is having an affair; someone who suffers from low self confidence and experiences social anxiety by believing other people make them uncomfortable; the distaste and dislike we have for a person who we deem ugly, slutty or fat which is actually veiling our own body image issues. We all project in our daily lives to protect ourselves against uncomfortable emotions, thoughts and perceptions that we judge as being too "bad," "ugly," "shameful" or "uncontrollable." When we are willing to reframe these projections and access what they are pointing to about ourselves we can begin to free ourselves from the binds of judgement and move into the more peaceful realm of self acceptance.

By reframing rascals into teachers, we shift our perspectives from pushing back to drawing in, as we attempt to understand what our teachers are showing us in their mirror reflections. With mindful awareness we learn to take a step back, breathe, center and then go inward to address what needs tending to. As we learn and grow, and adjust our lives accordingly, our mirrors will change. People will continue to come and go from our lives, if we are mindful of our interactions and irritations, and learn from them, each new wave of people will bring a new issue to light. This is a better alternative to the question, "why does this always happen to me?"

Breaking the Ties that Bind
This exercise will help you to start to shift away from the disempowering nature of your triggers to being empowered by them. Think of a situation in which you are repeatedly triggered and then start to break it down. First figure out what exactly is the trigger: is it a button, pothole or rascal. Then ask what is the prominent negative feeling that arises. Write your answers down. Next explore what needs are not being met in this situation. Try to discern the specific words, behaviors and situations that seem to trigger you. Analyze the data like a detective and look for the patterns. In time, this exercise of observation and introspection will make you more aware of your emotional reactions. With practice you will start to be able to see how your reactions are just smoke screens to cover up the real issue, which is you.

As you begin to see the emotional needs that are not being met, and in turn, are unconsciously directing your behavior, start problem solving to figure out how you can meet your own needs. You may discover you have a strong, dependency-like need to be approved by those close to you. Or you might realize that you can't stand to lose someone's respect. Or maybe you feel intimidated by people with a high social or professional status. Each of us has a unique combination of specific needs and vulnerabilities when relating to others. Knowing and understanding your needs is an important step in learning to reframe your stories and get back into the driver's seat of your life. Eventually you will come to a place where you do not rely on anyone else for your happiness; you realize it is an inside job. If you need approval, start working on self acceptance. If you feel insecure, start appreciating your strengths and assets. It takes time and consistent effort, but reframing your triggers will dramatically improve your sense of contentment with your self and your life.

Journal: Rewriting Your Story

Take a piece of paper and draw a line down the center. Start to list on the left side of the paper all the people and/or situations in your life that cause you to have a negative emotional reaction. You can use as many sheets as you need. After you have exhausted your list, on the right side of the page imagine what lesson you might take away from this situation and what actions might be called for to help shift the negative energy.

Here are some examples of the struggle, and possible reframes:

1. *Frustration with income level.* Perhaps you could revamp your resume, start looking for new employment opportunities. Or start working on a creative venture on the side like crafting or writing a book. Maybe consider going back to school or creating a budget.

2. *Feeling lonely.* Perhaps you could explore new groups or organizations such as church or MeetUp.com. Or adopt an elderly neighbor who could use some help around the house and would enjoy some company. Join a gym or social group.

3. *Complaining about partner or family.* This opens a real opportunity to look at your life and timeline and consider what it is you really want from your relationships. You could start a dialogue with your partner/family about what you are learning in this book and invite them to share their thoughts. Therapy is another wonderful avenue to start observing yourself and how you relate to others from a more objective point of view.

4. *Feeling out of shape and overweight.* Enlist friends and coworkers to become work out buddies or create a "Biggest Loser" contest. Perhaps this is an opportunity to explore cooking and nutrition and take it upon yourself to get some guidance on how you could change what you are eating and reframe your relationship with food.

Once you have completed both sides of your list, cut it down the middle and throw away the left side. Put the right side somewhere you can see it everyday. Start working on one situation at a time and begin incorporating small goals each day that will move you closer to your reframed vision of the problem. For instance, if you want to tell a different story about your diet, make it a priority one day to consciously choose foods that are healthier for you. Remind yourself of the reframed story throughout the day by saying things to yourself such as, "I am consciously choosing to eat healthier because I want to feel healthier." Or "I am proud of myself for taking the time to take care of myself today by eating well."

Rewriting our stories takes time and patience. Take it bit by bit, because if you try to change too much too fast it will feel overwhelming and you will not be able to sustain the momentum. Get creative in telling different stories. Some stories will be very easy to change, and some will require more effort, but everything in your life is up for negotiation once you realize all you need to do is start telling a better story.

Meditation: Creating a Safe Space

The purpose of this meditation script is to help you to create a peaceful, safe place within. This place may be a real or an imagined space that you can return to at any time to help calm your mind when you are feeling triggered. As you first start working with this meditation, it is important to set aside at least five minutes a day to go to this space. Remember with meditation, it is all about practice. The more you practice, the more your brain will change.

To begin, find a comfortable sitting position. For the next few moments, focus on calming your mind by focusing on your breathing. Allow your breathing to center and relax you. Breathe in.... and out. In..... out.....imagining as you exhale, that you are releasing any tension in your body. Feeling your muscles relax, bring your focus to any areas that feel tight and invite them to release on your next out breath. Let the rate of your breathing become gradually slower as your body relaxes.

Now begin to create a picture in your mind of a place where you feel completely safe. It can be a favorite place in nature, either at the beach or in the woods, or an imaginary place, where you feel calm and relaxed.

Start with the physical surroundings you are imagining. Where is this peaceful place? You might envision somewhere outdoors....or in-doors. Really bring into focus all the physical elements of the space you can imagine. What time of day is it? Are you alone or is someone else there with you? Are there animals, birds, plants, or water?

Are there relaxing sounds around you in your peaceful place? Imagine any tastes and smells your place has to offer. Bring to mind the sensations of touch, including the temperature, any breeze that may be present, the surface you are on, and the position of your body. Are you sitting or lying down? Imagine the details of this calming place in your mind.

As you bring into great focus this space imagine a feeling of calm, of peace, of creating a space where you have no worries, cares, or concerns. A place where you can rejuvenate, relax, and enjoy just *being*. Once you have all the particulars of the space in mind, take some time to enjoy this space. Breathing in and out, in and out. With each in breath drawing in the peace of this space and with each out breath letting go of any tension, tightness or negativity.

Know that you can return to this place in your mind whenever you need a break. Remember, the mind does not differentiate between the real or the imagined, so at any time you can give yourself a virtual vaca-tion, and reap the benefits of the relaxation. The more you practice, the quicker your body will respond to the images.

In these last few moments of relaxation, create a snap shot in your mind of this safe place that you can return to the next time you need a quick relaxation break. Focus on one aspect of the image, perhaps a pine cone, or a crashing wave, or the feeling of comfort from your bed. This will be your starting point each time you want to return to your peaceful place.

When you are ready, turn your attention back to the present. Notice your surroundings as your mind returns to its usual level of alertness and wakefulness. Wiggle your fingers and toes to wake up the body. When you are ready, slowly open your eyes and continue on with your day.

Creating Your Ultimate Story

We cannot control what happens to us most of the time, but we always have control over how we respond. If you perpetually feel bothered, depressed, or grumpy, you are repeatedly telling stories that cloud your vision of life. Learning to understand the triggers that elicit and perpetuate these emotional states is a powerful reframing tool. Those terribly irritating people can become profound teachers. Those mannerisms in others that drive you mad become an opportunity to surrender control, practice patience, or just embrace compassion. All our triggers become an invitation to look within and determine where you have slipped into a story line, losing touch with the present moment.

The take-home is this: what situations do you see repeatedly coming up in your life that drive you crazy? How could you apply the "soft overcomes hard" approach and change the way you see the situation? Move from frustration to compassion, from anger to passion, or judgement to acceptance. Knowing when you are triggered is a perfect time to mindfully put on your curious glasses, take a step back from the situation to inquire about what is really going on. This creates space to reframe the story, to redirect your focus away from rationalizations and to point rather, towards growth and understanding. Like being an investigative reporter, we start to see there is an underlying truth beneath all of the crap that we throw up as a screen to cloud our vision of what is really going on. When we open our hearts to the truth, we are offered an opportunity to accept ourselves and others to just be who we are.

Shifting from the things outside of us that seem to get in our way, we now move into our stories themselves. In this next chapter we will begin exploring the specific stories we tell ourselves by pinpointing what has been passed down to us from our families of origin, and what developed along our own personal timelines. We can start to see how these fabricated stories have come to shape the life we are living today.

5

What's Your Story, Morning Glory?

"My life has been filled with terrible misfortunes, most of which never happened."

Mark Twain

"You will see it when you believe it."

Wayne Dyer

I am Not Smart Enough

"You should really consider a trade school, Lara, as I'm not sure you will succeed in college." These are the memorable words of my high school guidance counselor. She meant well, I am sure, and was only going on the facts she had in front of her, as she was counseling me on my future. I had repeatedly started school from the 5th to the 10th grade in the gifted and talented classes only to be taken out and put in general classes mid-year as I was unable to keep up with the work. I was graduating smack in the middle of my class as far as my GPA was concerned, with a GPA of 2.7 something. I had been unable to break the 900 mark on my SAT, after two tries. This score was even after taking the SAT review course my mother doggedly drove me to every Saturday morning for weeks and taking the practice test twice. My record did not bode well for a successful college experience.

Fortunately for me, my mother was determined to see me go to college as she filled out my college applications and heavily assisted with the essay portions. Because of her efforts, I did get into college, had a year of scholarly success, and then found myself performing on an average level once again.

My senior year in college I recognized that if I was going to realize my dream of medical school I needed to start getting serious about my future. Up to this point my college career was dictated by the easiest path possible. I had dropped psychology as a major because I could not pass statistics and I avoided any difficult classes like the plague. My senior year I signed up to take chemistry, lasted about a week, and then dropped out. I had a panic attack the first day in class as I was overwhelmed by the material and the nagging belief that I did not belong in the class because "I was not smart enough". I completely chickened out, and gave up on my dream. I graduated with a degree in Sociology, or as my father liked to say, I majored in "unemployment." Well, unemployment it was for me for the next decade.

Seven years later found me depressed, stricken by an eating disorder, and working as a bartender while living in my mother's garage. One evening I met a neighbor at a family gathering. She was talking about her daughter and how she was working on being accepted into the Physician Assistant program at James Madison University, my alma mater. I had heard about PA school from my brother who was a paramedic. He kept encouraging me to look into PA programs after each monumental MCAT (the entrance exam for medical school) failure but I was too wrapped up in the story that I had to be a doctor to be able to listen.

In my conviction that I knew what was best for me, I could not hear my brother's very wise advice. I kept hitting my head against the wall of medical school admissions and with each failure, reinforced my belief that I was not smart enough. It took hearing about PA school from a veritable stranger to pique my interest. The woman was so proud of her daughter for her ambitions and her enthusiasm was contagious. That single 10 minute conversation was all it took for me to be able to re-frame my story enough that I could start to peer outside of my very self-limiting box of beliefs and consider taking a risk for something I truly wanted.

Over the next several days, I had a few good self-talks. I knew I need-ed to do something or else my life would continue along the same trajec-tory it was on and that scared me. If you had asked me at 17 what my life was going to be like, I would have whole heartedly told you I was going to marry my high school sweetheart, be a stay at home mom and raise a family. Well, it did not work out that way so I had to consider Plan B. I applied to the JMU Physician Assistant program, and was accepted. That was a pivotal moment for me because the people in charge of this program thought I was smart. And with this acceptance the self limiting story that I had subscribed to for 27 years began to crumble, and slowly, over the next two years of PA school, I began to see how much I had held myself back by believing a story that was so clearly untrue.

This was the single largest turning point in my life and it all hap-pened because I was brave enough to challenge a very old, self-limiting story about myself. "I am not smart enough" became, "I am open to infinite possibilities." This chapter is for anyone who can relate to feel-ing as if they are their own worst enemy, and who wants to learn how to reframe their own story to glimpse the realm of unlimited potential.

Storytelling and Mankind

Storytelling is the oldest form of narrative communication known to mankind. Every human culture throughout history has created stories as a way of making sense of their world. Even before spoken language existed, humans told stories using signs, drawings and sounds to relay important information about food sources, or dangers to be avoided. Stories help us from a very young age to make sense of our environment and understand our roles in our families and communities. They provide structure and direction as we navigate the challenges of life, making sense out of the chaos and creating security out of unpredictability. Through the associative links stories bring, they help us to feel that the world makes sense.

However, there is a downside to our reliance on stories. They trap us in a box of perception that colors the way we see the world. From the time we are born we hear stories of race and sex, power and victimhood, all which influence the creation of preferences in beliefs and values. They unconsciously affect every decision we make, and determine how we view our lives. The Radical Reframe process is about identifying these stories, getting curious about where these stories came from, how they shape your life, and then reframing them to bring out the best possible outcome.

Our core stories are created in childhood. We come out of the womb wired for stories because they make learning and remembering easier. The young brain grows at an astounding rate, reaching 90% of adult volume by age 6 years old with structural changes continuing through out childhood and adolescence. This process begins to slow down in our early 20s, and the way the brain sees the world is pretty much solidified by the time we turn 25. What is experienced early on in life creates the foundational framework through which the brain functions when we become adults. This is why it is so important to look back on the stories our family of origin taught us about the world, for they are the lens through which we see our lives.

Studies of military veterans and PTSD reveal those who experienced trauma as children are more likely to develop the symptoms of PTSD, as compared to those who did not experience trauma as a child. This research underlines the tendency of the brain to create associative patterns in response to intensely emotional experiences. The imprint of trauma in childhood predisposed the soldiers to developing PTSD because they already had created neuronets of associations with painful emotional experiences that were carried into adulthood and onto the battle field. When brains are exposed to trauma during the rapidly growing stages of brain development, they are more sensitive when reexposed as adults because the brain is able to recognize the pattern of what is happening whereas a brain that has not experienced trauma, does not. The traumatized brain automatically recruits the established neuronets of alarm to go on high alert and start secreting stress hormones in response to the situation while the soldiers without the preexisting experience of trauma do not have an associative story to fall back on, and therefore have a better chance of moving on after the incident with no lingering effects.

Luckily not everyone has experienced significant childhood trauma, but we all have lived through painful emotional experiences as a child. Whatever it was that you experienced as a child, the situations that elicited strong emotional reactions created pathways for stories that became the foundation through which you see the world. If you had parents who tended to view life as a glass half empty, or you did not have enough positive experiences to balance the negative, the negative stories you were told will cloud your view of life. If someone who experienced trauma was raised in a loving and supportive family, they may move forward remembering the story but not have that negative emotional wound shape their life. When families are able to give the gift of security, stability and positive self regard, children are more likely to create a more positive outlook of the world, and one that involves feeling safe, secure and confident. If we did not receive these gifts from our families we grow up believing the world is not a safe place.

The Power of Story

There is a very old Taoist story of a farmer who lives in a poor rural village. The farmer was considered well-to-do because he owned a horse which he used for plowing and transportation. One day the horse ran away. The neighbors proclaimed it was a tragedy, but the farmer just shrugged his shoulders and said "maybe." A few days later the horse returned and brought with it two beautiful wild horses. The neighbors rejoiced in his good fortune and the farmer just said "maybe."

The next day the farmer's son was thrown from one of the horses and broke his leg. All the neighbors were distressed over the farmer's bad luck, but the farmer again said "maybe." A few weeks later war broke out in the country and every able-bodied man was drafted and sent to battle. The farmer's son was unable to go because of his broken leg. When the neighbors told him how lucky he simply replied, "maybe."

This story demonstrates how easily our moods can fluctuate if we rely on our external environment to dictate our state. The meaning of any event depends on the "frame" in which we perceive it. When we change the frame, we change the meaning. Having two new horses seems like a good thing until the son breaks his leg and can no longer help with the farm chores, which could be perceived as a bad thing. But in the context of the son being drafted and becoming a soldier, it appears good. We see how the villagers experience a roller coaster of emotions almost daily based solely on the stories they make up about the farmer's fate, while the farmer remains neutral. We all have this ability to stay steady in the turmoil of life, we just need to be mindful of our emotional reactions, the stories we tell and the direction we wish to go in our lives.

Most of us have never considered that the stories we tell ourselves are perhaps not serving our highest good but instead perpetuating old, dysfunctional patterns of belief. For example, if you grew up in a family that was continually worried about money, and you grow up believing that there is an inherent lack of resources in the world. You will constantly be looking for proof of lack of resources in your life to validate this story. We can take this example a little further and say, if you believe you have to struggle and work hard just to make a living you may be more inclined to stay in a low paying job than looking for a job that better compensates your efforts. This is how the brain works: it creates narratives that support beliefs that have been formed out of past experiences. To continue supporting these stories the brain will look for proof in your current world for what it believes. If you believe life is hard, you will see evidence that life is hard. If you believe life is fulfilling, you will see evidence of fulfillment in your life. As crazy as it sounds, whatever you believe will come to fruition in your life because what you see is predicated on your expectations.

The good news is that the opposite is also true: if you grew up with a parent afraid of poverty and yet you started focusing on stories of abundance, you will see proof of abundance in your life and begin to make choices that make you feel more abundant. You see this story line all the time in the rags to riches stories of movie stars, politicians, or business moguls who came from nothing and created empires. For a great example of the subjective nature of stories consider the meaning of success. Some people will live their entire lives and never feel successful, yet have a good job, a house, and a healthy family. Another person may feel like a complete success each time they put their feet on the floor in the morning with no house, no job or family. How can both be true? How can the definition of success be so different for each person? How do you think the meaning people attribute to success contributes to the satisfaction they feel in their lives? The difference between success and failure is just a reframe away, so why not start creating more stories of success?

The Strength of the Family Narrative
The first 20-25 years of our lives create the foundation of our beliefs and expectations for adulthood. How we were treated as children shapes the foundational story of how we treat ourselves and others. The quality of the interactions we had with our caretakers and the messages they gave us about ourselves and our environment set the stage for all relationships to come as they shape the stories we tell ourselves about the world and other people. As our lives become more complicated with the demands of adulthood - hectic schedules juggling family, work and self time -- we generally don't give much thought to the fact that we are creating our lives around the family narratives we inherited and we rely heavily on this early programming to navigate through our adult lives. We are unconscious of how we are reacting in-the-moment during most situations in our lives as we have our awareness somewhere else: constantly pushing forward onto the next thing. Because

our behaviors feel so familiar to us, as we have spent our entire lives observing them in our parents and now in ourselves, we assume they are normal. The thing is, everyone is walking around assuming their behavior is normal because they have a different narrative running in their brains.

The only time we tend to stop and consider our automatic responses and the stories we tell is when we experience great pain. At those times in our lives when we are brought to our knees by life, here is where we might ask "Why do I keep dating the same type of person, or losing a job, or spending all my money?" It is at these junctures that we have a reprieve from the fugue, and are open to change. Unfortunately, most people do not know what to do when sitting at the threshold of change, and so after the pain subsides, they go back to the same old stories and behaviors expecting a different result. The reason we continuously repeat painful behaviors is because we are acting unconsciously. We have an inkling that our behaviors are not in balance with our deepest desires, and yet the pull of habit is so strong we allow ourselves to go with the flow, not wanting to disrupt our lives or upset somebody else with true introspection.

In an ideal world, we would all have perfectly attuned parents who were able to teach us how to be honest and love ourselves. These ideal parents would have given us just the right amount of space and independence to flourish and fully develop our unique selves. In this utopian world parents would provide a solid base from which we could venture out independently as individuals and yet know we could return back when things get confusing or hard, as they helped us develop a sense of self-reliance and competence. Through their enduring support we would grow up feeling safe and secure. Parents do their best, but for most of us, "their best" emanated from an unconscious story they were taught by their parents when they were young. If we do not take the time to explore the dynamics of our families and the stories we were taught as children, we are destined to repeat what we learned, and as a consequence, find ourselves trapped in the patterns of our parents.

Amanda

This truth came out very powerfully in my work with a young woman named Amanda. She was coming to see me because she did not feel she loved her husband and questioned whether she ever had. As Amanda explained, "I realize my whole life has been about being secure, and now I am feeling like I have everything I could ever need but I feel empty inside." As we explored her timeline and discussed the rules of her family, an interesting story about secrets came out. Although she had not thought of this situation in a long time, she remembered that she had known from the time she was a teenager that her mother was having an affair. In fact her mother had confided in her about the affair because she did not have anyone else to tell and she begged my client not to tell her father.

Because of this experience, Amanda grew up in a household where the primary story of marriage was about secrets. When she asked her mother why she stayed in the marriage her mother said it was because she could not afford to leave which cemented for Amanda the belief that marriage was about financial security, not love. The feeling Amanda was having towards her husband was a direct consequence of the messages she received from her mother and father about marriage.

This was her a-ha moment: with this new-found awareness, Amanda could see she did not know what a loving marriage looked like. She shared with her husband what she had learned about her family of origin and then together they went onto marital therapy to begin reframing their marriage. This is a great example of how our primary care-taking relationships set the stage for our lives. These relationships in effect define the expectations we have of our own lives: from work to marriage, to friendship and parenthood.

The stories we inherit help us to exist within our family system. They are a type of survival mechanism. The problem comes when we grow up to believe they are the only way of seeing life and adopt them as Truth. The thing is, there is no absolute Truth, but we cling so tenaciously to our inherited belief systems that when we are confronted with a different, perhaps even contradictory story, we feel threatened rather than curious. These stories we cling to are so familiar to us we don't even notice them as habits of thought, and as a consequence miss out on all the opportunities we have to see things a little differently and appreciate different as good.

The Stories We Tell

Self-empowerment is a feeling of confidence in knowing you have the ability to take charge of your life, that you can trust your own instincts and be your number one cheerleader. When we feel self-empowered we know we are responsible for who we are and the direction in which our lives are headed. Empowered people are self-aware and able to clearly identify their values, strengths and weaknesses, recognizing areas that need work; their inner narrative is supportive of growth and understanding.

Disempowerment is a universal feeling of being deprived of power, authority or influence to make changes in one's life. We become disempowered by the thoughts and beliefs we have that are negative and judgmental. Every time we reinforce a disempowering story we rob ourselves of our own free will. When we believe what others say about us, and have internalized a story of our lives based on others' expectations of us, we have no power.

The Radical Reframe process is about starting to look at our stories and behaviors and the outcomes they produce as a way to gain insight into all the places we unknowingly lose our power. This is a process of looking for disempowering patterns and themes in our lives, and then with introspection, discovering where they live in our stories. A great analogy is how electrical appliances when plugged in silently drain energy and cost us money but we are unaware of it. Once we are able to shine the light on the origin of the pattern, we offer ourselves an opportunity to take our power back by actively constructing a new story. I want to highlight three of the most common disempowering stories I encounter in my work: perfectionism; the need to be right; and victimization. Sound familiar? Well read on to see how these stories are robbing you of your life.

Our Quest to Be Perfect

One of the most prevalent - and damaging - stories in our culture is the *need to be perfect*. This belief in the story of perfection begins early in life as we were given praise and approval by our caretakers for being good, obeying orders, doing as we were told, and not making waves. Our education system reinforces this belief through a rigid grading system: children are trained to achieve based on standards created for them to succeed in life. As we grow and integrate this story of perfectionism into our world view, we become sensitive to criticism, and fear making any mistakes. Perfectionism thus becomes ingrained in the very fabric of our culture, being continuously reinforced in our families, the workplace, and society in general.

Perfectionism has many setbacks. The first and foremost is the stress created by constantly living in fear of making a mistake. Because of this fear of failure, people are hesitant to investigate the unknown or test their own identities. It keeps people from engaging in challenging experiences and exploring their creativity to solve problems. Perfectionism reduces playfulness and the assimilation of knowledge; if you're always focused on your own performance and on defending yourself, you can't focus on learning a task. It also reduces efficiency as we have created such a rigid template for learning and working. And because it lowers the willingness to take risks, perfectionism reduces creativity and innovation: which leads us to another self-defeating story called *being right*.

I love the quote by Wayne Dyer "Would you rather be right or happy?"

I remember when I first heard those words I was like, "What?" That made no sense. If I'm right, then it is very important that others understood this, and know that they were wrong! Geez, after all, if I were wrong, I'd want to know, right?

Wrong.

Being right or wrong actually has nothing to do with being right or wrong. It has to do with being good and accepted and directly plays into our self esteem. Our need to be right usually is an indication that we are not feeling so great about ourselves. We think that being right makes us better, and when others are wrong, that makes us superior to them and in control. The problem is if we are right and the world is wrong, we not only limit our ability to expand our knowledge, but this story also alienates us from others. The very fact that we'd mindlessly choose to win an argument at the cost of damaging our relationships points to something terribly amiss. Pride and ego are what make it imperative to be right, at the cost of intimacy, understanding and compassion.

Changing how we see the world can be one of the scariest things we ever do. A truly open mind is not afraid of being wrong, because to truly hear other points of view helps to expand our own awareness and cultivate greater compassion for the human experience. Indeed it is by fully listening to other points of view that we can be open to growing and learning new things. Arguing with someone about who's right is a waste of energy and time, and often ends in frustration. After all, when was the last time you convinced someone to change their way of thinking by arguing with them?

I encourage clients to start monitoring their need to be perfect and right. When they catch themselves correcting other people, interrupting their stories or just flat out saying "you're wrong" I give them a few tips to try to start reframing the need to be right. First, remind yourself that we are all perfectly imperfect human beings. No one has all the answers and each of us is on our own individual path, so we cannot possibly know what is best or true for another person. Choose to trust that people act based on what they believe is best for them. Remember that whatever another person thinks or says does not diminish your value, and sometimes if we are open to listen to opposing beliefs we may change our own beliefs. Practice a willingness to be flexible in your behavior and commit to keeping your heart open; you never know when an idea or belief will dramatically affect the path of your life. Remember how my mother's neighbor's admiration for her daughter's desire to go to PA school radically changed my life?

And so I would pose to you this questions: how much suffering are you willing to cause yourself and others with your need to be perfect or right? It is an interesting thing to consider. And remember there are many people who have dramatically affected the course of the world by being wrong many more times than being right. Consider these epic "fails": one of Beethoven's first teachers called him a "hopeless composer"; Walt Disney was fired by a newspaper for lack of ideas; the movie Star Wars was rejected by every major movie studio in Hollywood before 20th Century Fox finally produced it; Thomas Edison was both hearing-impaired and fidgety and he lasted only three months in school where his teachers said he was "too stupid to learn anything." (Edison was eventually home schooled by his mom). In talking about his invention of the light bulb, Edison said: "I have not failed. I've just found 10,000 ways that do not work." Edison was obviously a gifted reframer.

I believe the Radical Reframe of perfectionism is giving yourself a break and allowing yourself to let go. Not everyone will be able to do things exactly as you expect, and you shouldn't expect that they do. Releasing the story of perfectionism allows us to sit in wonder of all the differing ways humans view the world. By letting go of expectations and allowing people be who they are and do their thing, we give ourselves, and others permission to learn, grow, and shine in the perfectly imperfect act of being human.

The Blame Game

We are all guilty of playing *the blame game* at some point in our lives. The one where your job, your wife, your dog, your mother-in-law, your neighbor six doors down, the media, the government, the receptionist at your doctor's office, or the tailor who measured you incorrectly is somehow responsible for the problems you're having now. We blame because we don't want to take personal responsibility for whatever is causing our negative feelings: if we took responsibility that would mean we had a hand in causing all that does not make us feel good. In essence, blaming or pointing the finger at someone else is saying that we are absolving ourselves of having any responsibility in the matter -- whatever it may be. By feeling we are a victim, our unconscious attitude is: "I am not responsible for my plight." Thus, we create a story of someone else being in control, which strips us of all our power.

On the surface it seems rational to blame someone else for how we feel. I mean, if they would just do what we want them to do, or not do, then we will feel happy. Right? Wrong! Every time we blame someone for how we feel we are giving away our power. We are in essence telling them they are responsible for our happiness, and if they do not act accordingly, it is their fault we are unhappy. This makes us the victims of circumstance. By pointing the finger of blame, we miss out on the opportunity to experience our own humanity - to be open to vulnerability and feel what it is like to be loved and accepted with all our faults.

Happiness is an inside job, and if we walk around believing our happiness is the responsibility of our parents, spouses and friends we are destined to be perpetually disappointed by life. This is where reframing can be so pivotal to creating a happy life. Instead of pointing the finger of blame outwardly, each time we feel the urge to do so, just turn that finger around and point the finger back at yourself. Be introspective and ask yourself what you might be trying to avoid by pointing the finger of blame at someone else. It is as easy as that. I know it's not really so easy because there are a million reasons why we can blame the world for our unhappiness, the problem is, how much does blaming actually make you or anyone else feel better? Uh, never. But if we can reframe the story and realize we are the only ones capable of changing the situation by altering how we interpret what it means, then we get our power back and know we can be happy no matter what.

Here is an example of taking ownership of your feelings by reframing blame. Try substituting "I'm pissed off because you never consider my feelings" with "I get upset when you cancel plans with me." This easy turn-around puts you back in the driver's seat. It not only de-escalates the situation but also invites the other person into a conversation. The person we are engaging with has a choice, they can either be interested in why our feelings are hurt and work with us to resolve the issue, or not. At this point you can decide if you want to keep this person in your life. By holding a space for your feelings and then honoring them by asking for what you need, you begin to trust yourself to get your needs met in a healthy way. If your friend responds with respect and kindness, you know they can be trusted in the future and decide to keep them close. If they are insensitive and don't seem to care, you can choose to put some distance between you and them, recognizing they do not have your best interests at heart. The empowerment comes from recognizing you have a choice, you always have a choice, and if something doesn't feel good, it is your responsibility to do something about it.

Lastly, here are some tips to help you stop blaming and start taking responsibility for your life. First, trust that there is a lesson to be learned in every situation and strive to learn it. Put your curious glasses on, get out of your own story and look for all the possibilities to see the situation differently. Take responsibility and admit to yourself you co-created whatever problem has arisen. Take a moment to consider how you contributed to the current situation. Then, take some alone time to process the situation. You can use journaling or talking to a close friend, just make sure you tell the truth and not your version of the story. Once you have seen where your story took over from the present moment, start reframing the event by releasing blame, accepting responsibility, and acknowledging what you would like to change. Releasing blame and accepting responsibility is very powerful. It opens us up to healing and the power of unlimited possibilities.

Liz

Liz had been working with me for two years to treat her depression and anxiety, and came in to my office one day an emotional wreck. After a few moments of silence the torrent rolled out. Her husband was having an affair with his ex-wife. She kept repeating over and over again, "how could this happen to me?" "What am I going to do?" She spent the session blaming him for all her pain and ruining her life. This session was primarily damage control: allowing Liz a safe place to emote and explore her feelings of betrayal and abandonment.

Once the initial shock was over, we set to work reframing the situation, beginning with how Liz contributed to the situation. With the assistance of her timeline and journal, she was able to see the resentment she had been harboring for the past 10 years since her husband had his first affair. "I guess I never really forgave him and kept punishing him for what he did." We started to dive a little deeper into her past and uncovered fears of abandonment she had from growing up with a father who was in the Navy and often deployed overseas while Liz was left at home with a mother who suffered from severe depression. Liz came to see she had a profound fear of being abandoned but also felt guilty for leaving, which is partly why she did not leave after her husband's first affair. Her story about her being responsible to make everything okay, as she had felt when she was a little girl and had to care for her younger siblings when her father was away and her mother was depressed.

After discovering these deeply set behavioral patterns, we started to reframe the story of what next. We looked at her options: try to work it out; leave amicably; or duke it out in a bitter divorce. In the end Liz decided to walk away gracefully. She first forgave her husband and herself for all the things that caused pain in the marriage. She asked for what she felt she deserved, and because her husband did not feel attacked, he was open to mediation. There were some tense negotiations, but after a year of processing Liz walked away feeling sad, but also empowered to create a new life for herself that was more honest and authentic.

Getting Honest

One of my first spiritual teachers used to always say, "Isn't this curious?" when I would babble on about my husband's hurtful behavior. In the beginning I would retort, "Of course this is not interesting, this is terrible." But soon I began to see her point. Asking "isn't this curious?" allows us to take a step back and glimpse the bigger picture. I have taken this approach a little further and will pose to clients in the midst of their emotional angst, "Isn't that curious, is it possible that..." as I offer a perspective that is slightly outside the realm of their understanding in their heightened emotional state. This is the first step in starting to get honest with ourselves about what is really going on and the stories we have created that cloud our vision.

Shakespeare was onto something when he said, "To thine own self be true." The more we are able to be honest with ourselves - and the people around us - about our feelings, we begin to realize we can take care of ourselves and feel safe in our vulnerability. Here is the caveat: we cannot expect those who do not give us what we need to wake up one day with the realization of the error of their ways. When people show you who they are, do yourself a favor and believe them, take what they offer at face value and decide if that feels good for you. Adulthood is about realizing we are free to surround ourselves with anyone we choose, but in order to do that we MUST be honest with ourselves and those around us about what we need, feel and believe.

One of the most significant ways we surrender our personal power is by believing a story that *we somehow owe other people something*, that we are responsible for their feelings or happiness, and that we are protecting others by hiding our true feelings. In the end, this tendency to hide our true desires, feelings and needs is what fuels relationships clouded with unkind words, criticism and judgement. For when we are not honest with others, we lose the potential for intimacy and intimacy is what gives us a sense of connectivity to other people and the human race. When we choose to hide, we choose to feel isolated, lonely and misunderstood. Our fate is of our own making. A good example is my client Amy.

Amy

Amy came to me for help creating healthier boundaries. She knew she had a bad habit of over-extending herself and felt frustrated not having enough time for herself and her family. She was constantly overbooking herself, and then when she realized she could not possibly do all she had agreed to do she would fudge her reasons for cancelling and then feel guilty for lying. As we sifted through her stories and timeline, a pattern started to emerge. Amy had a primary belief that she would be missing out on something very important if she said no. The irony is, by over-committing she never really could say yes, because her guilty thoughts would cloud her ability to be present for whatever she choose to do over all her other commitments.

Amy's timeline revealed many instances as a child where she would anxiously look forward to something, only to have something ruin the event. One such example is Christmas morning, and Amy's mother drinking too much the night before and throwing the Christmas tree out of the house. Her mother's drinking problem ruined many things Amy had looked forward to as a child. And so, she created a story that if she committed to everything that came her way, perhaps this next time would be the one that would be great. But overbooking diluted her attention: when she overbooked she couldn't get too excited about any one thing because she felt too anxious knowing she had to choose which activities to cancel. This helped her avoid her true feelings of angst and fear of being disappointed.

Amy worked on getting honest with herself as well as her friends and family: she forced herself to call each person to tell them honestly why she was cancelling. Amy has been able to be more mindful of her time and commitments as she learned that the pain of disappointing the ones she loved was worse than the discomfort of saying no. By learning to work with her feelings, and heal some of the unmet needs of her childhood, she has been able to have more realistic expectations of people and events, and recognize that there is an ebb and flow to life. By being present she can find something gratifying in almost every situation.

Journal: Honesty and Timelines

I would encourage you to take some time to journal about the ways you are not honest with yourself or others. What little white lies do you tell, or what information do you omit from sharing with other people? When do you minimize your feelings or exaggerate your response to someone else to make them feel better? Explore what honesty means to you and some of the reasons you omit the truth. What does honesty mean to you? Create a journal entry where you imagine yourself completely free to be your authentic self. Outside of judgement or scorn, what would your life feel like? What would you do? If unrestricted by expectations, how would you make sure you got your needs met? What would you ask for, what would you do differently? Really dig deep into what you need and explore what that might look like. It can set the framework for the new story of honesty in all areas of your life.

When we are courageous enough to be honest with ourselves and others, we develop a strong sense of self worth and confidence. This is not to be confused with arrogance. An honest person knows their strengths and weaknesses and can see such in another person. When you have a strong sense of self, you know you are a valuable, worthy person, independent of what other people think. You don't feel the need to be judgmental of others because you are secure with yourself and therefore grounded in acceptance of yourself and other people. This joy that comes with emotional freedom is ripe for the taking if you can learn to start being honest with yourself.

Timelines help us to understand our own personal history. Each one of us has a personal timeline that began the moment we were born. This timeline consists of highs and lows represented by the positive and negative experiences we have had, all of which have come together to create the person we are today. Putting this timeline on paper is an excellent way to record your life cycle, the main events and patterns will start to reveal themselves and show how they created the life you are living today. You begin to see the evolution of thought patterns and beliefs through your timeline, places where story lines were created and reinforced, as well as turning points where you may have started to see things differently.

To create your timeline, get three pieces of paper and tape them together lengthwise. Start with your birth on the far left side of the page, draw a line across the pages and end with your current age on the far right side of the page. Think about the major events in your life, both good and bad, and start to map them out. One client put all the "good" things above the line and all the "bad" things below which helped her to see the positive and negative patterns more easily. It does not matter how you do it, personalize the timeline however you would like. No event is too small or insignificant to put down: if it comes to mind, write it down. Mark down any significant moves, changes in friends, illnesses and achievements. Patterns will start to show up in all areas of your life. You will get a bird's eye view of your beliefs around money, work, family, friends, church, neighbors and how these beliefs are shaping your life now.

Some questions to ask as the timeline evolves might be: Do I see any patterns in what happened to me as a child and what is happening to me as an adult? What stories might I have adopted from my parents that I can see in my life now? What's my part in this pattern? What belief system is perpetuating this situation whether it be at work, home or within the story of my finances? How might I be misconstruing a situation to fit a story rather than being able to see the entire situation for what it is? Are there any repeating patterns in my relationships, my work history, or my home life?

As you begin to recognize patterns from your time line that are showing up in your life, you can start to see opportunities to dive deeper into the origins of these patterns to find the driving story behind the behavior. In chapter 7 we will explore the art of reframing these stories so for now just sit with the insights you are gaining from this exercise. I love working with timelines, because they are so ripe with insight and information. Like peeling an onion, there are always deeper layers to uncover, and more work to do, so keep at it. Remember, the rewards in life are in the journey, not the destination.

Meditation: Daily Redo
When you close your eyes to go to sleep, take a few minutes to review your day. When you come to an event that was less than ideal, or aroused a negative emotion, bring the circumstances of the event to mind. Imagine as many details as you can -- the time of day, where you were, who you were with, what was said or done. Then, using your imagination, create a different story. You can change anything about the event as long as you stay connected to your emotions, and feel how the changes shift how you feel. The goal is to feel satisfied with the event before you go to bed so you don't take the negative emotions into the dream world. For the brain cannot tell the difference between what is real and what is imagined, especially as the brain is preparing to go to sleep, so if you go back and rewrite the event, the brain will just carry an abridged version into sleep.

This is especially helpful after a bad day. Really invest in creating the outcome you want, as fantastical as it may be. Another useful variant of this exercise is considering alternative reactions to situations you might come across again in the future. I imagined calmly facing my raging husband many times in my mind before I was able to do it in reality. I would reimagine a negative event, with myself maintaining my composure and speaking calmly but clearly about my needs and expectations. All the while preparing myself for the time when I was ready to change the old story and create a new one. Each time you rehearse a better ending you enhance the possibility of shifting your story when that situation arises again. This is one of the most powerful tools in your reframe chest.

Wrapping Up

In this chapter we looked at how the power of our stories shape our lives. Because the human brain is wired to follow and create stories, our lives are dramatically affected by the stories we learned, we believe and repeatedly tell ourselves. The tales we tell hold powerful sway over our memories, behaviors and even identities. They shape our thoughts and beliefs and directly influence the path our lives take. They are our identity. Every story we tell is a gift or a curse depending on how we frame it. So, I challenge you to start looking at the stories you tell and question how they might be shaping the story of your life.

Now that you have a good understanding of mindful awareness, the value of your emotions, and the power of your story, we move into the realm of personal integrity and self respect by exploring boundaries. Those invisible fences we set up, ensuring relationships are mutually respectful, supportive and caring. Boundaries are a measure of self-esteem. So let's dive into exploring your boundary system and see where you might need to do a little fence mending.

6

Boundaries: Where You End and Others Begin

"No one can make you feel inferior without your consent."

Eleanor Roosevelt

"Daring to set boundaries is about having the courage to love ourselves, even when we risk disappointing others."

Brene Brown

Tim's Introduction to Boundaries

Tim was an upper level manager for a family owned nursery. He came to me at the insistence of his pain specialist as medications had not helped his worsening lower back pain and she believed a large part of his discomfort was coming from stress. Things in Tim's life seemed pretty normal when he talked about his marriage and children, but once Tim started talking about work he would become very agitated.

Tim was overwhelmed by his work life. "My co-workers are like children. I am constantly having to help them and tell them how to do their jobs. My work suffers because of it." As he described his daily routine it became clear that Tim felt he was personally responsible for everybody else's performance. Tim had been an employee for the company since he was 15 years old. After 30 years, he knew the ins and outs of the business but what Tim never learned was how to manage people. Because he had basically grown up in the business, the work relationships had felt more like family, rather than business. This made it hard for Tim to feel comfortable correcting people's work or asking for things to be done differently. Therefore, he spent most of his day following up on his employees and making sure things were done correctly.

As a consequence, Tim was overworked, overstressed, and starting to feel resentful. Over the past few years, this resentment started spilling over into his family life and physical health. Tim notes that his back pain began soon after his most recent promotion — about 5 years ago. As we mapped out his time line he started to see the relationship between stress at work and exacerbations in back pain. The biggest indicator that something needed to change at work was when he went on his last vacation and after being away for 2 weeks he returned almost pain free, only to feel the pangs of discomfort well up as soon as he walked in the door of his office building the first day back.

Tim started to notice real changes in the quality of his back pain after we started talking about creating healthy boundaries in his workplace. He began to see how he needed to let his employees do their jobs, while simultaneously building trust in his employees that the work will be done and done correctly. Tim began recognizing the need to set firm consequences for substandard actions, and relinquish control to let his employees be responsible for their own work. It was not his job to make sure they did a good job, it was his job to let them know what the expectations were and then follow through on the consequences.

At first this was very hard for Tim because he worried about how the negative consequences would affect the families of his employees as well as the business. We worked on cultivating an understanding that everyone is responsible for their own choices and behaviors. If someone makes bad choices, it is their responsibility to live with the consequences. In the end, those people who made bad decisions were perhaps not the right type of employee for the company. Tim came to see that every time he compensated for another's poor performance, he was in essence giving the employee permission to have bad behaviors.

Once Tim started to understand that most of the work he was doing was not beneficial to him or his employees - and in fact, in the long run, he was hurting the company because he was not able to do his own job well - he went to work educating himself on how to be a better manager. He started attending management conferences, learning how to let go of control while supporting his employees to grow and develop at their own pace and in their own way. He started developing more mature and supportive relationships with his employees and found he got more satisfaction from his job when he was able to trust his employees to do theirs. By setting up clear expectations for his employees, Tim was able to take a step back and let his employees have the space to make and own their choices.

After about 6 months, his back pain had dramatically improved, due in part to the fact that having one job was much less stressful than the ten jobs he was doing previously, and also because Tim now had time to take care of himself. He started going to the gym and was able to get home for dinner at least three times a week. Once he was able to create healthier boundaries at work, Tim started to feel happier, and less weighed down by the burden of everyone else's work. He lost weight, started to feel good about himself again, and his relationship with his family improved. This is a great example of healthy boundaries at work. Let's start exploring what these things called boundaries are and how they help you reframe a happier, more balanced life.

The Importance of Valuing Self

Simply put, boundaries are where one person ends both physically, emotionally, spiritually and another begins. In the physical world, boundaries are easy to see: fences, signs, walls, moats, lawns, and doors are all physical boundaries. They are signals to those on the outside looking in where they can go and where they cannot. Personal boundaries are not so concrete. They are fluid and flexible, like a fence with a gate and we are the gatekeepers. Ultimately we are responsible for whatever we allow into our sphere of influence.

Personal boundaries provide guidelines. They are invisible rules or limits that a person creates to identify for themselves what are reasonable, safe and permissible ways for other people to behave towards them. They also help to determine appropriate consequences if someone ignores or steps over those limits. Healthy personal boundaries boil down to this: taking responsibility for your own actions and emotions, while NOT taking responsibility for the actions or emotions of others. We are responsible for everything inside our boundaries, someone else is responsible for everything outside of our boundaries.

Each way we interface with our environment constitutes a boundary. Physical boundaries pertain to the body and the surrounding space. Whom do you touch or allow to touch you, when and why? How do you feel about things in your environment that affect you? Noise, activity, light? Mental boundaries apply to thoughts, beliefs, values and opinions. Are you easily influenced or very opinionated? Can you listen to opposing ideas with an open mind or are you rigid in your thoughts and beliefs, unable to listen to opposing views? If you are highly argumentative or defensive you most likely have weak mental boundaries. Internal boundaries dictate how we manage ourselves from the inside, from our diets to exercises regimens, to our emotions, thoughts, behaviors and impulses.

Emotional boundaries come from having a good sense of our own self-worth. They make it possible for you to separate your own thoughts and feelings from those of others and to take responsibility for what you think, feel and do as we allow others to do the same. Healthy emotional boundaries prevent you from giving advice, blaming or accepting blame. They protect you from feeling guilty for someone else's negative feelings or problems and taking others' comments personally. High reactivity suggests weak emotional boundaries. Sexual boundaries protect your comfort level with sexual touch and activities. People with healthy sexual boundaries understand it is their right to determine all levels of sexual interaction from conversations, to touch to engagement with another person. In the end, boundaries are all about regulating our relationship with ourselves.

Understanding Poor Boundaries

Many of us struggle with poor boundaries. If, when we were growing up we were shamed, ridiculed or bullied for asking that our needs be met, we will create a story that we are "less than" or "not worthy" of love and attention. We may even create a story that we are selfish when we put our needs first. These beliefs evolve into a greater story of feeling responsible for how people see and treat us as well as feeling it is our job to make people happy. Many times, out of fear, we will adapt to other people's needs and wants, taking the focus away from our own needs, and placing the priority on other people. When we do this our energy becomes divided and ultimately we lose the thing we strive for the most: our happiness. You can never make another person happy; you can only share the happiness you have with the world.

Here are a few questions to assess the integrity of your boundaries. Don't worry if you respond yes to most of these, in fact, give yourself a big high five for starting the journey of cultivating self respect by creating healthier boundaries. Do you have a hard time standing up for yourself? Do you keep agreeing to do things that you don't really want to do? Do you tolerate rude comments or pushy people because you are uncomfortable with conflict? Do you take things too personally? Do people say you are overly sensitive? Do you say yes because you feel guilty or no because you feel responsible? If you said yes to any other these questions you may struggle with personal boundaries so read on to hear what you can do to build better fences.

Where Did You Learn to Draw the Line?

This is the golden rule about boundaries: you are responsible for your own happiness and everyone else is responsible for theirs. Boundaries provide clarity. You see, in order to establish boundaries, you must be clear about what you want, what your beliefs and values are, and in essence, have clarity about who YOU are.

We need boundaries in order to have healthy, fulfilling relationships. They define who we are in relation to others and help to maintain our own personal power and energy. Boundaries are how we know "this is who I am." They are how we show people how we would like to be treated and create order and predictability in our lives. We gain a clearer sense of self and are able to trust life freely when we maintain healthy boundaries because we know we are able to take care of ourselves no matter what happens. With healthy boundaries we are able to take full responsibility for our lives as we learn that we are the ones who determine how we will be treated and what type of energy is acceptable to be around. We gain trust in our ability to take care of ourselves, protect ourselves from harm and pursue situations that feel good to us. All this results in a healthy sense of empowerment.

When we don't have healthy boundaries life feels scary and unpredictable. This contributes to feelings of anxiety and depression, as we do not feel we have control over our circumstances, and these circumstances define how we feel. Having a sense of boundaries and limits helps you to connect with your true self. Your boundaries are based on your beliefs, thoughts, feelings, decisions, choices, wants, needs, and intuitions. When healthy they are clear, firm, maintained, yet flexible. When we don't protect our boundaries our needs go unmet which causes us to over-give, over-commit or over-accommodate.

We primarily learn boundaries from our family of origin. Those with poor boundaries were generally raised by caretakers who had poor boundaries themselves. These caretakers were not as focused on helping the child develop into a mature independent adult but instead relied on the child in some way to get their own needs met. We are unable to develop a healthy understanding of our own boundaries if we felt responsible for someone else's feelings when we were a child. Whether by being blamed for our father's outbursts or feeling we were responsible to make our mothers happy, we learned that our job is to take care of other people's needs. Our parents do their best, and we as parents do our best, but if we were not taught what it means to have healthy boundaries we cannot pass on this valuable life skill to our children.

As adults, the messages we learned from our parents become our way of life. For how could it be any different? We will repeatedly find ourselves in unhealthy relationships, jobs and life situations if our early lessons about boundaries were less than ideal and our feelings, views, and opinions were not respected within the family. But it doesn't have to be this way forever, learning to reframe your stories and create new healthy boundaries takes practice and patience, but it can be done! And it will lead to a healthier, happier life.

The Art of Cultivating Healthy Boundaries

Knowing your boundaries is really about self-awareness. The more you can be aware of what you are feeling, the more sensitive you become when your boundaries are being violated. Your emotions are like a warning system to boundary breaches. When we feel angry, anxious, irritable, annoyed, all these emotions are generally pointing to the fact that an internal or external boundary has been crossed. There are many ways in which boundaries are violated. External boundary violations have to do with physical space like standing too close, unwelcome touching, or behaving in too familiar a way. Internal boundary violations include things like taking responsibility for someone else's thoughts, feelings or behaviors. When someone assumes how you feel, think or what you should do, they are violating your internal boundaries as well as when someone tells you how to conduct your life or tries to manipulate you into doing what they want.

Here are some good questions to consider that will help clarify the perimeters of your boundaries. What do you need from other people to feel safe? To feel respected? To feel valued? Answering these questions is a way for you to start defining boundaries. Notice that these are fundamental needs we all share: the need to feel safe, respected and valued. Creating healthy boundaries is about figuring out how to satisfy your needs within your relationship with yourself and others through honest and clear communication.

Here are some other important things to remember when creating healthy boundaries. First and foremost make YOU a priority. Take some time to identify your physical, emotional, mental and spiritual limits. Consider what you can tolerate and accept what feels uncomfortable and inappropriate. Then start figuring out how what your imaginary fence is going to look like.

Once you have established the perimeters of your boundaries you have to learn how to defend them. Fear, guilt and self-doubt are the most likely pitfalls of having weak boundaries. We may fear another person's response when we enforce our boundaries. We may feel guilty for speaking up or saying no. We may doubt that our needs are more important than others' needs. Recognizing this discomfort is all part of the process. It's not enough to create healthy boundaries; you must be prepared to defend them, which can be very uncomfortable, especially if you have a strong story line of being a people pleaser or being uncomfortable with conflict.

It is crucial that we learn to be direct and assertive when we are communicating with other people about what is important to us. Let other people know in a respectful way what is bothersome to you and then be open to work together to address the issue. Get support if you need it. Whether this comes in the form of a support group, church, counseling, coaching or just with a trusted friend, be courageous enough to turn to someone else for help to clarify what is happening and determine what you need. With friends and family you can even create a conversation about boundaries and make it a priority to practice setting boundaries together and working to hold each other accountable. This is ideal because you all know each other's stories, because you are operating on the same software, so working together to change shifts the entire family story, affecting past and future generations.

Creating healthy boundaries is about loving yourself enough to create a new narrative to reframe your life stories so that you come first. The tools you have learned of mindful awareness, coupled with the understanding of your most common stories will help you determine what feels good and what does not. With this information, you will have a road map to follow to explore your boundaries and discover where they are weak. Remember boundaries aren't just a sign of the health of your relationships: they're a sign of self-respect. So give yourself the permission to set boundaries and work to preserve them. Good and bad things will happen, but with a centered and balanced heart, we can get over any obstacles. Next we will explore one of the most common and pervasive examples of poor boundaries: co-dependence.

Codependence verses Interdependence
Codependency is characterized by sacrificing one's personal needs in order to try to meet the perceived needs of others. It is associated with low self-worth and insecurity and typically reflects having a dysfunctional relationship with your self. The primary stories associated with codependency are: the need to please other people; a reliance on external validation for good deeds; and seeking approval that comes from caring for and rescuing others. These people are the great rescuers in life. Whether it is an over-involved mother or bossy friend, they feel responsible for other's reactions and emotions. The problem is, no matter how well-intentioned, this behavior boils down to a way to try to exert control over another person so they feel better about themselves.

Because codependents usually have a hard time saying no, they are often seen as people pleasers. Codependence leads to seeking approval and validation from others which robs a person of their own self respect. People with codependency issues rush in to take care of other people, often at the expense of their own self-care. It is natural to feel empathy and sympathy for someone who suffers, but codependents put other's needs ahead of their own. They may even become upset or offended if someone rebuffs their attempts to help; they will take it as a rejection of themselves, not recognizing that someone else is defending a boundary of their own.

When people exhibit codependent behaviors, they most likely grew up in a family that was very chaotic and unpredictable, and as a consequence, try to control the people and circumstances around them to feel some sense of security. Because their needs were not attended to as a child and were not often met, they either do not know what they need or desire or are afraid to speak up for fear of repercussions. This is the most damaging aspect of being in a codependent relationship, because if you do not know what you need and cannot be clear in communicating your needs to other people, you will constantly be feeling unhappy and unsatisfied with your life and your relationships.

Interdependence on the other hand refers to the quality of people with healthy boundaries engaging in relationships that are balanced and mutually reliant. Each person is working to have their needs met but also to ensure the needs of their partner are being met as well. *Codependence* is about establishing self-esteem by taking control of all the things outside of self whereas *interdependence* is aligned with taking responsibility for what is on the inside and then having mutual respect for the other party. Interdependence is a healthy way of relating because each person is involved in the other person's life without sacrificing their own needs and values. People in interdependent relationships recognize the importance of keeping their own identity outside of the relationship and feel confident in expressing their opinions while still being sensitive to the other person.

Interdependent relationships require effort, nurturing and healthy boundaries. Gaining awareness of your own needs and goals is an important step toward reciprocity in relationships. Making a conscious decision to compromise or make a sacrifice for another person can be a positive thing as long as it doesn't undermine your sense of self and well-being. The reframe from "I am responsible for everything" to "I am responsible for myself and expect others to do the same" will radically change your life for the better. Surrendering the need to control other people provides the necessary space to appreciate the strengths and weaknesses of ourselves and others: it creates the foundation for healthy and satisfying long-term relationships.

Setting Personal Boundaries
Living with healthy boundaries creates a sense of security in our lives, it promotes healthy intimate relationships, and is a sign of self respect. Healthy boundaries mean we have the freedom to be who we are and we allow other people to do the same. We can let go of trying to control situations and learn to accept whatever situations arise, knowing we will know how to take care of ourselves, regardless. When we have unhealthy boundaries we tend to derive our self worth from others and external situations, and this leaves us disconnected from our inner wisdom.

It takes time, support, and relearning to be able to set effective boundaries. Self-awareness and learning to be assertive are the first steps. Setting boundaries isn't a selfish act. It's self-love; you say "yes" to yourself each time you say "no" to something that robs you of your power. It builds self-esteem. It is our responsibility to take care of ourselves, and with healthy boundaries we protect ourselves when it is necessary. We can always have empathy for other people but we are never responsible for them or their behavior.

Remember that people will react to you when you start setting new boundaries. As you change your behaviors and expectations, it will affect other people and how they have been interacting with you, which sometimes can feel jarring. It is important to remember you are not responsible for another person's experience. If they do not ask for clarification about why you do the things you do, or turn to you in anger when they feel you have hurt their feelings, then they are the ones with the problem and you cannot help them with it.

The best place to start is getting to know yourself. Get clear on your likes and dislikes, start to notice the people who seem to increase your energy and feeling of value and then the ones who seem to take your energy and drain your self-esteem. Notice what activities boost your positive assets and what activities trigger your self-judgement. Learn to appreciate the things you are good at and start becoming selective about the people who you spend your time with. Remember you are the only one who is going to start reframing the choices you make to create a healthier internal and external environment.

Try out these tips to start you on your way to creating and maintaining healthy boundaries: get clear on what is and what is not acceptable to you; own your feelings and don't blame them on anyone else; set up consequences for bad behavior; and lastly, let go of the outcome. You are only in control of you, unless you have children or pets, and then you assume some responsibility for their actions, but in adult-to-adult interactions you are only in control of your actions and what you allow to happen. If you don't like what happens, leave, hang up, move out or speak up.

Remember, you have a right to your feelings and boundaries. In the end we must take responsibility for how we allow people to treat us and stop making up stories to justify poor boundaries. Our boundaries act as filters, permitting what is acceptable *in* and keeping what is not acceptable *out*. Have you ever heard the phrase, "you can only give away what you have"? If you do not respect and care for yourself, you cannot take care of anyone else. As adults, the only person responsible for our health and well being is us. And by taking responsibility for our happiness we also give permission for others to do the same.

Learning to say "no" is one of the most difficult things we can learn, but it is a gift we give ourselves. As a society of people pleasers, many of us go to great lengths to accommodate everyone. We are terrified of appearing selfish, and therefore agree to things that don't feel good to us. In reframing "no" we are actually saying "yes" to ourselves, to being committed to our own health, wellbeing and happiness. Being *selfish* is actually a very healthy thing to do, because it gives you the power to choose where you invest your energy and your time. This act of selfishness will bring the best rewards for all parties involved.

Learning to speak up is also a necessary component of creating healthy boundaries. Let others know when you feel they have acted inappropriately, overstepped a line, or made you feel uncomfortable. Don't be afraid to tell others when you need physical or emotional space. Be true to yourself at all times and speak up when you feel others are trying to change or control you. Know what actions you are willing to take if your requests are not heard or your boundaries are repetitively breached.

Healthy boundaries make it possible for you to respect your strengths, abilities and individuality as well as those of others. Trust and believe in yourself. You are the only person who can be an expert on you and you can never be an expert on someone else, so stop trying. Get honest with yourself about your strengths and weaknesses and know your limits. Figure out what you need, want and value; stop turning that power over to anyone else.

Journal: Get Clear on Your Boundaries
Start an inventory list of all the relationships you find emotionally up-setting and why. Explore relationships where you feel your energy gets drained or you feel they are disrespectful to you. Write out the reasons why you continue to maintain these relationships. Then start reframing the scenarios. If your sister continuously calls to complain about your mother and this is upsetting to you, imagine that you could establish a healthy boundary by saying something to the effect of: "I hear that you struggle with your relationship with mom, but I find it upsetting when you call and complain to me about her. I would appreciate it if we could avoid talking about your issues with her." If your sister continues to talk about your mother after you have set a clear boundary, then you need to consider what the consequences of her choice might be and run through some options in your journal so you are ready to act if need be.

This exercise is so valuable because it is like a dress rehearsal. The more you practice the more likely you will be able to honor your boundaries and defend them when needed.

Here are some examples of boundary setting statements that you might use:

- Yes I can help you as soon as I've finished with this task.
- I want to hear all about your day, I'll be free to give you my full attention in 15 minutes.

- I'm sorry I can't bake cookies, I already have a commitment with my family.
- You're welcome to live here while you are going to school as long as you follow our rules.
- I'm not willing to argue with you about this.
- I'm not willing to talk about this situation right now.
- When you do _____, it makes me uncomfortable, I would like for you to stop.
- When you say _____, I feel _____, can we come up with a different way to say it?
- I'd be happy to discuss this with you when you are able to speak in a calm manner.

Each of these statements is emotion-free, and clarifies a boundary in a completely neutral manner. It is your job to clarify your boundaries and when you feel they are violated, it is your job to defend your boundaries. This journal exercise can be a very valuable tool to help you learn how to state your boundaries and then know what to say if you need to defend them. Please know it takes time and practice, so if you are not fully able to get your point across the first time you try, bring it back to your journal. Sift through the story to get to the truth about what you need and then reframe the situation. Setting boundaries is about respect - respect for yourself and respect for other people. Boundaries are not about arguing, fighting, name calling, blaming, causing guilt or shame. They are about honesty, and intimacy. So when you are writing out your boundary setting dialogues, make sure you keep the emotions out of it. Facts only please.

Meditation: Creating Your Own Personal Force Field
I love this meditation because it gives you a visual representation of what boundaries might look like. I like to call it my force field meditation because it is like being a super hero with an invisible force field and only you get to decide what gets in and what stays out. To get started, find a comfortable seat. Start focusing on your breath. Feeling the breath

come in and out, invite your body to start to relax. Imagining with each in-breath drawing in positive light and energy, and with each out breath imagining letting go of any tension, toxins or tightness in your body.

Once you feel centered imagine you have a force field around your body. Notice the texture, color and size of the field. As you imagine the force field understand that only you are in control of what gets inside and stays outside of the force field. The force field is there for three reasons: to keep things that are not true *out*, to let things that are true *in* and allow things that are not clear to hover right on the edge. Here is how it works.

Bring to mind a situation that elicited an emotional reaction from you. Consider the situation and what triggered your response. Consider the trigger and whether it was based in fact or fiction. For instance, if someone said something to you that was not true, visualize this statement bouncing off the force field, never to be considered again. Or perhaps someone lashed out at you in anger and called you lazy, and you know for a fact that you are not lazy, then poof, that accusation is gone and you never have to worry about it again. This aspect of the force field is self protective as it helps you screen out the the things people say to you or lay blame on you but are not your responsibility. It gives you permission to completely let it go.

When someone says something that is true for you, the force field allows it to come into your space for you to consider and work on. The force field may take some of the reactivity out of the statement, because you recognize it as true and desire to learn from this valuable information. There is nothing to defend or react against when you are actively choosing to utilize information given. For instance, let's say your boss comes to you and says you dropped the ball on the last project you did. You may initially feel defensive, but you can acknowledge you did not give it your best effort because you had some big family obligations that got in the way. So, because this was true, it slips through the force field into your space so you can work on it. Perhaps next time asking for help, or talking to your boss in advance of the deadline to explain the situation.

The most valuable component of the force field meditation is when something is said to you and you are not sure if it is true or not. If something is said that may have some truth in it, it is held at a distance for you to consider. For example, if your friend angrily says something like "since you've been dating Jeff you never call me." Your first reaction might be to push back with anger and deny the accusation. But with the forcefield meditation, you can imagine the statement hovering just outside of your field as you consider carefully whether or not it is true. If there is some truth to the accusation, you can allow that statement in to your field to consider and decide what you want to do with the information. Perhaps apologizing for your behavior and asking your friend what she feels she needs. If it is not true, you can let it go.

This force field is a visual metaphor for you to understand that you do not have to accept or respond to all the energy that is directed towards you during the day. Most people are unconsciously directing negative energy at other people as a way of deflecting their own feelings. Instead of taking responsibility for their feelings and processing them, they project them onto someone else. When this happens you do not have to take on the negative energy. In fact, if you allow it to pass you by with no reaction, the person who sent it will be stuck with the energy again. As in the example I gave with my husband, when I reacted back with anger, the angry energy escalated between the two of us. It was like I got hooked into his anger and agreed to be angry too. But when I reframed the situation, and chose to remain calm, he was stuck with his feelings of anger with no reprieve because I did not agree to do an angry dance with him anymore. I just let the anger he directed at me bounce off my force field.

The more you practice this force field meditation, the better you will be at recognizing during emotional times what is true and needs to be worked on and what is fiction and needs to be disregarded. We carry around so many stories that are laid on us by other people, and when we have unhealthy boundaries we accept them as our own burden. Your life will feel lighter once you can learn to let go of what is not yours and more effectively manage what is.

The Gift of Self-Containment

Boundary setting is hard work. In a world that rewards an attitude of control, manipulation and avoidance, we are taking the path less traveled by reframing our lives to respect ourselves and others by being honest about what we need and feel. It is important to understand that boundary setting is not a rude or selfish act, but is a necessary practice to create peace in our hearts and cultivate intimacy in our lives. Without boundaries we are not only adrift in a sea of other peoples' expectations, but we are also at the mercy of our emotional whims. When done in a positive, respectful manner, boundary setting increases assertiveness and communication, and enhances trust between two people.

Remember this is a process, so be patient with yourself. Healthy boundaries will not magically appear overnight. As you learn to reframe your stories and expectations, new needs and desires will arise. It is like peeling back the layers of an onion: with each new layer there are new opportunities for growth and personal understanding. Seek feedback from people you love and trust, and direction from others who you feel have healthy boundaries. Most important of all, value your feelings, for feelings are never wrong! It is the stories we surround them with that cause us pain.

Now we move into the application of all that we have been learning up to this point: we will be putting these components together to give you you life examples of how to turn around the stories that you tell...to radically change your life.

7

The Reframe: The Art of Self Empowerment

"You have to begin to tell the story of your life as you now want it to be and discontinue the tales of how it has been or of how it is."

Abraham-Hicks

"Whether you think you can, or whether you think you can't, you are probably right."

Henry Ford

Allen's Story

I worked with Allen for about a year. He was sent to me by his wife to deal with his anger management issues. He felt a great deal of shame over his behavior, but did not know how to stop it. He noted that by the time he got home from work he had no patience left, and just wanted some peace and quiet. As we started to look at the triggers and situations that activated his anger, Allen started to see that he was way too stressed at work, and was bringing that stress home to his family. Allen had the expectation that coming home at the end of the day should feel like a relief, but in actuality it would feel like the opposite. Allen's expectation that his family could make him feel calm was like expecting an enjoyable kayak ride in a hurricane.

We started with his expectations of home, and where they came from in his life as a child. With this understanding, Allen was able to reframe his expectations to be more realistic when he walked through his front door. We then brought his kids and wife in on the conversation of what would be most helpful for dad so he can relax after a long day and not feel the need to explode in order to have some peace and quiet. After he was able to understand and relay his needs to his family, a conversation started about creating realistic expectations for the family when dad got home. Everyone got to express what they needed: his wife needed to feel supported, his children needed to be seen and have some fun time with dad, and Allen needed to feel he could relax and do some things for himself.

Together Allen's family worked out a timeline for the end of the day, where everyone's needs were met. They posted the timeline on the fridge, which really helped Allen anticipate expectations of him when he got home, and this, in turn, reduced his irritability. Everyone understood there might be last minute changes to the schedule, but with the expectations clearly defined, each member of the family felt heard and valued and that their needs were being addressed.

Once we had some structure in place in his external environment, we then worked with Allen on reframing the messages he was getting from his emotions. Allen had a father who would regularly yell, which explains why it was hard at first for Allen *not* to go into his automatic response of anger when he was feeling overwhelmed. The story here is "if I yell loud enough everyone will shut up and leave me alone." With mindful practice, Allen began to notice when he was getting worked up and irritable and use it as an indicator that he needed to take a break and practice reframing. He started using the tools of stopping, centering, inquiring and reframing to help diffuse his habituated pattern of getting angry. After a few weeks he noticed his stress levels began to

significantly subside at home but also at work as he was able to let things
go and address his own needs in a healthier behavior of self care.

The Radical Reframe process helped Allen to use his awareness of
feeling overwhelmed and irritable as a signal that he needed to address
a need that was not being met. Allen was a perfectionist and put a lot of
pressure on himself at work. With mindful awareness, Allen was able to
start using the Radical Reframe process to notice when he was getting
worked up, take a step back and do some breathing exercises or stretch-
es to clear his head of the story that was building up with the irritation. Once he felt he was centered again, Allen would get back to work.
Heretofore, Allen's pattern would be to hold it all in and push through
with unrealistic expectations of himself and his work, ignoring his feelings until he got home where all his frustration would come spilling out.
Learning to be aware of, and take care of, his own feelings and needs
at work took the pressure off his family waiting for him at home. Allen
now looks forward to going home, spending some quality time with his
children, helping to support his wife and then savoring a little time for
himself before going to bed.

What are You Feeding?
There is a famous Native American story that demonstrates well the
power of choice in our thoughts. An old man and his grandson are sitting by a fire outside of their tepee, wrapped in furs and gazing into the
leaping flames. High on a snowy ridge, a wolf howls at the moon and
another answers from far away. Soon after, the old man removes the pipe
from his mouth.

'Grandson,' he says. 'There are two wolves inside you. One is white,
the other is black. The white one is all the good qualities of the heart:
love, compassion and kindness. The Black one represents all of the negative qualities of the distorted heart: jealousy, anger and fear.

'What are they doing there, Grandfather?' asks the wide-eyed boy.

'They are fighting for control of you,' says the old man.

The fire crackles and sparks flare in the night. The wolf on the ridge
howls again and the old man puffs contentedly on his pipe.

Finally, the boy says, 'Which one will win, Grandfather?'

'Ah,' says the old man, 'The one that wins is the one that you feed.'

This story illustrates how we always have an opportunity to reframe a situation. We cannot take away the pain or grief or disappointment that life will present, but we can reframe our response into an understanding that whatever comes into our life experience is rich with information. We can always choose to feed the white wolf. We never have to let our negative emotions dictate how we behave or how we see the world. A reframe may be an invitation to dig deep into the essence of our being and explore forgiveness, compassion, acceptance...or a reframe may be a call for better communication, or a call to create more clearly defined boundaries.

We have all seen people go through what appeared to be a terrible situation only for it to turn into a dramatic blessing. A painful divorce opens the opportunity to find true love 3 years later, or a job lost enables someone to start and build a thriving new business. The powerlessness we feel in our lives is just an illusion - a self defeating story we choose to believe that renders us incapable of making the dramatic changes we need to create the life we want. The Radical Reframe process shifts that feeling of helplessness into an understanding that you ultimately have the power in any situation if you do these four steps: stop, center, inquire and reframe.

We unconsciously reframe meanings all the time based on circumstances. For example, a squeaky shoe on a busy sidewalk has little meaning, but the same sound outside your bedroom door when you are alone in the middle of the night elicits a completely different physiological response. A squirrel scampering around the yard appears cute; a squirrel tearing through your house appears to be a terror. It is all in how you frame it.

The Radical Reframe process encourages us to access our creative sides; it gently invites us to expand our perception of what *is* into what *could be* possible. This process will alter the trajectory of your life. Look at it this way, a simple reframe of thought could be seen as a 1 degree shift in a path. At first a shift appears to make little difference, perhaps a degree or two in your life trajectory. But one year out it is now a 30 degree shift and 5 years out it is a 90 degree shift, and eventually the path is completely new. This is the power of changing our thoughts, one small shift will radically change your life.

Utilizing the Radical Reframe process literally changes your physiological response to situations. You learn to see the potential for passion in anger, the victor in the victim. As you shift your stories your brain chemistry shifts right along with you. Remember, your physiological responses are due to your perception of what is going on, not actually what is happening.

A great example is how people react to dogs. The same dog can be lying quietly on the ground minding his own business. As people walk by they display a myriad of reactions. Some may walk right on by and not even notice the dog -- experiencing no feeling at all -- some may feel the thrill of seeing a dog and want to pet it, and some will experience fear and walk across the street to avoid the encounter all together. What was different in each of these situations? Each person had a different biochemical reaction based on the story they believe about the dog, which lead to varying experiences even though the situation remained the same. When you perceive or anticipate something stressful, threatening or harmful, your body will respond by activating a chemical cascade that perpetuates a fight or flight response. When you perceive a pleasant situation, your brain will respond by releasing a flood of feel good chemicals, to include dopamine and serotonin which are responsible for the warm heart, and a relaxed sensation.

Okay, let's put it all together and start exploring the Radical Reframe process. The four step process goes like this: stop, center, inquire and reframe. It is as easy as that. I am going to break it down into four parts so we can explore what each process means.

Step 1: Stop
As humans we spend a lot time thinking about what was and what could have been as well as what is going to happen. While we are mentally wrestling with our fears, judgements and concerns, our bodies are moving

through life on automatic pilot. We are so caught up in "what's next" we have little awareness of what's going on right now, relying on this automatic pilot to get us through the day. We wake up to alarms, drink coffee while putting on makeup, rush to work, eat while driving or working, rush home, cook dinner, get the family ready for bed and then collapse into the bed and wonder why we can't sleep. If this is your life please take a moment to consider how your brain is very much like a computer. When your brain is programmed to think about what's next or harp on what happened, when you try to quiet down to go to bed, your brain is still in what's next/what happened mode. This is the reason we have an insomnia epidemic right now, no one knows how to turn their brain off and unfortunately there is no shut down button.

Another negative component of automatic pilot is the never-ending cycle of controlling, judging and criticizing whatever seems to be getting in the way. We have little tolerance for the speed bumps of life. The catch here is that life is in the speed bumps. I have hundreds of clients come to me complaining of memory and concentration issues. They admit the only way they can make it through the day is caffeine, nicotine and/or Adderall to keep them awake and alert: all of which put the limbic system into overdrive. Remember, when the limbic system is activated you are in fight or flight, and therefore the brain's focus is self-protection, not remembering details of the PTA dinner or working out smaller problems of a grocery list.

For most, the reason people are struggling with these issues is not because they have a brain disorder, but that they are habitually not paying attention to what is going on right here and now. Living within the perimeters of their created stories of what is happening, feeling tossed about by their emotional reactions and completely out of control in their lives.

By actively stopping throughout the day and taking some intentional slow breaths to center yourself, you begin to create a pattern interrupt, a "reset" if you will: breaking the habit of "what if" thinking and creating a "what is" habit instead. Rather than seeing something that gets in our way as an inconvenience, we start to reframe the story into seeing it as something *that is inviting us back into the present moment*. A pattern interrupt can propel us into new meanings and understandings about ourselves and others. It gives us an opportunity to look at something differently, to stop, take a step back and reassess the direction we are heading, whether it be a thought process or a path in life. Most people choose to grumble and complain about having to break old patterns or habits, but the Radical Reframe process is about seeing these bumps and turns as opportunities to stop and look more deeply at what is happening in our lives and take ownership of what we have created.

Mindful awareness of the present moment is an absolutely necessary skill if you want to become an active creator of your own life path. It helps us to access how it feels to just *be* a human being without feeling swept up in the activities of a human *doing* all the time. Taking time to stop and drop into what is going on connects us with our authentic selves. It is the starting point which gives us the opportunity to choose how we are going to interpret and react to situations as they arise. With life speeding past us when we are on automatic pilot we rely on the brain to put things together and make sense out of our world so it can determine our response. We first have to stop and *see* what is going on in our lives before we can reframe it.

Step 2: Breathe

Without oxygen there is no life, and without breathing there is no oxygen. We must breathe to live. Think about it: breathing is the very first thing you do when you're born and it's the last thing you do before you die. It sustains life by providing oxygen needed for the metabolism and removing the by-product of these reactions. Your brain uses about 25% of your oxygen intake to fuel metabolic processes that result in brain function. The brain is one of the most important organs of the body because it controls all other functions that are needed for survival. Individuals who are able to take in more oxygen may also improve the functioning of their brains. They are able to process, retain and recall information more effectively and efficiently. So when we deepen our breathing we dramatically affect our ability to process information which is crucial when we are desiring to reframe our stories.

Through the interplay of the motion of breathing, the stretching of abdominal muscles and the activation of deep abdominal nerve complexes, deep breathing stimulates the parasympathetic nervous system. Remember, the branch of the nervous system which helps us rest and digest: in essence promoting a state of calmness. As we practice deep breathing, and slow down our respiration rate, we also slow down our heart rate, lower our blood pressure and relax our muscles. As the body relaxes, the level of circulating stress hormones activated during times of stress, gets reduced. Focusing on your breathing connects you to your body - bringing your awareness away from your thoughts and stories and and into the present moment. This is an essential component for reframing, as the more you can detach from your reactive thoughts and feelings, and drop into the present moment, the better able you will be to objectively see what is really going on and then decide how to reframe it to get the results you want.

I would recommend practicing mindful breathing multiple times a day. You can pair it with your stopping practice: set your alarm for every hour and when you hear the chime, stop what you are doing and start mindfully breathing. As you are breathing notice what is going on around you. Feel whatever is supporting your body, notice the time of day, the lighting, the people around you and what your environment looks like and most importantly, what you are feeling both physically and emotionally. As you develop a breathing practice you will start to see that the quality of your breathing reflects your emotional state: stress and fear perpetuate restrictive breathing patterns; chronic anxiety creates a shallow, rapid breath pattern that reduces the amount of oxygen absorbed, in essence suffocating the brain and body. The worst-case scenario is when we start holding our breath: this has devastating consequences for our health, and I can assure you, most of us do it everyday.

Most of us have never given our breath a thought. It is the miraculous thing about Breathwork. It becomes an effective tool in your mindfulness toolbox, and it can be utilized at any time. When I first started Breathwork I was astounded at how often I was holding my breath. In the beginning I set an alarm on my phone, every hour it would go off and I would check in on my breathing, noticing the quality of my breath, and take a few deep, centering breaths, then move on with my day. Eventually I began to see how subtle changes in my breathing were telling me something about my emotional state, and if I could take a few minutes to stop, and breathe, I could easily begin to calm my breathing, reduce my subjective levels of stress as well as check in to see what was going on around me and the story in my head that was causing me angst.

The end product of STOP and BREATHE is cultivating the Witness Mind. Each of us has this amazing ability to observe what is going on both internally and externally with a detached attitude of a witness. When we are able to stop and detach from what we are doing, invite ourselves to relax and then just observe what is going on, we become a neutral observer of our own life. The witness place inside you is pure awareness; it is the part of you that is aware of everything; noticing, watching, accepting, just being present, right here, right now.

The witness mind is actually another level of consciousness, just like the meditative mind. It coexists alongside your normal consciousness as a layer of detached awareness, most of us have just never been taught the value of this state of mind. But we have all had that feeling that we were observing some event in our life with a strange sense of objectivity. I hear clients refer to it frequently during traumatic events, such as car accidents or health emergencies, when the brain is unable to fully piece together what is happening because there is a dramatic pattern disrupt. We are able to see it unfolding with our vision, but the emotional impact has not registered yet because it is so out of the ordinary; the brain cannot keep up and so our emotions fall behind creating this feeling of objective observation.

Humans have this unique ability to be in multiple states of consciousness at one time, it is the gift of our advanced brains. In any experience there's the sensory experience, the story, and then there is your awareness of it. That's the power of the witness mind: the awareness of being aware. With the practice of stopping and breathing, you begin cultivate this centering practice. Witnessing is like waking up in the morning, looking in the mirror and noticing yourself - free from judgment or criticism - just observing the quality of being awake. This process of stepping back away from attachment takes us out of being submerged in our limited experiences and stories and lifts us up into a place of non-judgement. Once you understand that there is a place in you that is not attached, that lives beyond this physical world and its' judgements and expectations, you are free to create whatever reality you want. Accessing the witness mind puts a laser light beam on the self-defeating stories which hold us back and offers the illumination of insight to reframe our thoughts to create whatever life we wish to live.

Relax and detach, these are the components of step 2, Breathe. The more you can focus on your breathing, the more aware you will become of what is going on inside and outside of you. Our ability to be in the present moment, to be in our feelings and in our hearts, is where we experience our power, joy and enthusiasm. When we have this connection, we are centered. When we feel centered we are at peace, relaxed and receptive, and are able to understand that every moment in our lives is a combination of good and bad. You become free to move out of the confines of your story and into the realm of eternal possibility.

Step 3: Inquire
Self-inquiry can liberate us to see beyond all that we thought to be possible: to be free to imagine and to dream. The power of the inquiring mind opens all doors of opportunity. It gives us permission to leave behind all preconceived ideas about what is going on and gives us the freedom to imagine that all things are possible. Inquiry begins with a curious mind. Curiosity, at its core, is all about noticing things and looking for what is interesting. It's about recognizing and seizing the novelty in whatever crosses our path. When we are curious, we see things differently, we use our powers of observation fully and tap into our creative mind. Inquiry pulls us fully into the present moment, helping us to connect with feeling fully alive and engaged in life. If you have trouble imagining what curiosity looks like, just watch a child. Their entire lives are driven by curiosity as they learn about this new world they have become a part of.

We all are born as curious, trusting human beings. Unfortunately, as we grow we are given messages that the world is not a safe place. not to trust the world or the people in it. We are taught to disconnect from our own intuition and heart intelligence and to trust the facts. Through this process we divorce ourselves from our own inner knowing and look to the outside world to give us the perimeters of our existence. Self-inquiry offers an opportunity to step back and get free from these stories and start to tease out what and how these beliefs created the life you are living right now.

We can begin to create different meanings for our experience with inquiry. For example, anger may turn into a request for some inner work to address your needs better. Depression becomes a sign that feelings have been repressed and need to be expressed. Loneliness becomes an opportunity to find new friends or communities and self judgement turns into an opportunity to show yourself some self compassion. Everything has a turn around, we just need to change how we see things and switch from an automatic judgement to a curious mind that asks better questions.

Inquiry separates you from your thoughts. For as seductive as the story seems, *you are not your thoughts*. Negative thoughts just offer an opportunity to start to ask better questions. What is really going on right now that caught your attention? What story are you making up about the event? What are you feeling right now? What are you wanting to do? Binge eat, hit someone, say ugly things, run away, blame someone. Get really honest about what your initial reaction was to the trigger and then get curious about where this is coming from and where it is going to take you.

Let's return to the example of binge eating. Let's say you get home from a stressful day at work and feel this incredible urge to go straight to the freezer, pull out that half gallon of ice cream, grab a spoon and dig in. As you are standing in front of the freezer, I would encourage you to put on your curiosity glasses and ask a few questions before you partake in the glory of sugar and fat overload. You can inquire about the urge to overstuff yourself by asking: what is begging for my attention right now?

What feelings am I wanting to stuff down with food? Why do I want to punish myself right now? How will I feel after I binge? What needs and desires am I not addressing? Binge eating is all about avoiding our feelings and abusing the things that nurture and sustain us: food and our bodies. By taking a moment to just drop in and inquire, you begin to open an opportunity for internal dialogue about the behavior and how it affects you.

If you are unable to interrupt the momentum of a disempowering behavior in the moment, with inquiry you can at least commit to doing the behavior a little bit differently. Rather than doing it with shame and guilt, embrace the fact that you are choosing to binge eat. Grab the biggest spoon you can, sit in the middle of the living room and bask in your ability to binge eat like a pro. Reframing your thoughts while you are doing the action allows an attitude of self acceptance to slip in. This is something we deny ourselves when we have a negative narrative of judgement running while we are doing something that is harmful or disempowering. How can you possibly change your story about food if you perpetually judge, criticize and hate yourself for your behaviors when you interact with food? There is no happy ending if you continue to be your worst enemy. So reframe whatever comes, acknowledging that you are choosing to do this behavior and accepting the experience with open arms and love.

Here are a few more tips to help you bring the art of inquiry into your life, and using it to turn something around. Make a commitment to yourself that as soon as you feel a tug of anything -- resentment, irritation, jealously, judgement -- you will implement the first three principles of the Radical Reframe process, STOP, BREATHE and INQUIRE. Explore questions such as how is the story I am telling affecting my emotions? Am I exaggerating any component of the story I am telling? Is my perception of the story true? Is this story familiar to me and does it have any familiar patterns that I have seen in my past? How else might I see this situation? Then start to throw out some alternative ways of seeing the situation with the statement, "could it be possible that _____?" Some fill ins might be: could it be possible that I am wrong, exaggerating, reacting, being irrational, etc. It is all about being open to alternative explanations and letting go of thinking you are always right.

＿ ＿

Research shows that being curious in life is an important factor in creating health and happiness, as well as keeping our minds active and creative. Opportunities for inquiry exist virtually everywhere; we just need to develop our curiosity muscle to see it. Here are some easy ways to start practicing having a curious frame of mind. Go for a walk and look around you with fresh eyes: make it a game to notice something new about your home, your neighborhood, or something in your partner's appearance which you have overlooked in the past. When talking, strive to remain open minded to whatever comes up, let go of the need to control the conversation or judge the information. Commit to asking more questions and spending more time listening rather than talking. When driving, turn off the radio and actively participate in the driving process. Notice the cars, drivers, signs, even scenery as it passes you by. Stay aware of what's ahead and on the horizon. When working, look for opportunities to challenge yourself or go beyond what is expected. When exercising, notice the intricacies and sensations in your body as you push your muscles and your heart. Take a moment to think about the strength and endurance you are building with each movement. You can start by devoting 5 minutes a day to your inquiry practice and you will start to see your life in a whole new way.

When we make an act meaningful with our inquiry, we enhance the experience and strengthen the pathways in our brain that trigger contentedness and well-being. In fact, curiosity increases the release of the reward chemical in our brains, dopamine, so each time we are truly curious we get a shot of happy chemicals in our brains which in turn supports the notion that we are enjoying the experience regardless of what it is. Once you have established inquiry as a skill you can start using it in your tough relationships and interactions. It is a gift you give yourself that will free you from so much unnecessary pain and suffering, and open up a new world of ever-evolving opportunities to see something differently.

Part 4: Reframe

You create your reality. The day you accept this truth and take conscious control of your thoughts is the day you declare your freedom and begin to be the captain of your life. This will be the day you cease to be a victim of circumstance and instead become a conscious creator. You will free yourself from the bondage of the external world and all of its expectations and move into a world created around your inner needs and desires.

Our thoughts and beliefs are the lens through which we see the world. Like a movie projector, your thoughts are like the film moving through the projector that is your brain, and the image on the screen is what you see in your life. If you think thoughts of lack and failure, you will see proof of lack and failure in your life as projected on the screen. If you think thoughts of abundance and success, you will see proof of abundance and success in your life. Up to this point you have learned how to become aware of your body and your emotions. You have learned how to shift your state of mind using heart-centered meditation, and you have made a note of the triggers in your life and highlighted areas in your life story where you get stuck. Now we look ahead. Step 4 is all about where we want to go and what we want to create more of in our lives.

It is all about what *happens next*. The REFRAME is where we take ownership of our thoughts and work to create a story that is positive and supportive of what you want to create in your life, regardless of what is happening around you. If you want more love, perhaps the new story is one of compassion. If you want more success, perhaps you are being called to action.

Reframing is a tool used to consciously change your limiting beliefs and stories to help support your desired goals, beliefs and behaviors. By interrupting old disempowering thought patterns with new interpretations and perspectives of reality, our thoughts start to support more helpful and desired objective outcomes. Reframing is a skill that shifts

the meaning of events and circumstances into a different context that is more favorable and creates a more positive frame of mind. Instead of sabotaging yourself, these tools offer the opportunity to overcome your personal limitations, boundaries, fears and even trauma.

In reframing, we understand the situations do not change, we change. Our views of the situation are altered to empower better choices and beliefs. When we actively change our frame of reference, this changes how we perceive, interpret and react to things that happen in our lives. You become more resourceful, realizing you have the power to change anything in your life, even the worst events can become opportunities for growth and self-compassion. It is important to remember reframing is *not* about pretending there are no problems in the world or obstacles in our lives. The world is not a perfect place. Reframing offers us an opportunity to always be open to new perspectives and ways of seeing things, which expands the possibilities for finding better solutions and paths moving forward.

You can reframe anything. Just take a moment to assess the situation and then decide to give it a positive spin. Take washing clothes for instance. Instead of spending time and thought energy avoiding the task or ruminating about how much you dislike washing clothes or don't have time to wash clothes, reframe the thoughts. Focus on how it brings you joy to take care of your family, or how grateful you are to have clothes you love. Express gratitude for running water and electricity to make the job of keeping your clothes clean easier. Washing dishes becomes a soliloquy about how much you enjoyed dinner or love the feeling of warm water on your hands. If you can't think of something right then and there just turn it over to the universe and be grateful to not know all the answers. Even the smallest reframes will make big changes in your life. Just a minute of conscious corrective action can change the quality of an entire day.

Here are a few more examples of reframes I have heard in my office. "I'm not sure what the future will bring but I am hopeful it will be good, and if not, I know I can handle it." Or "I've faced many challenges before, and I've conquered them all. Plus things rarely turn out to be as bad as I imagine them to be, this will all work out as it should." Lastly, consider the example of the all-out self-blaming statement, "It's all my fault." Sometimes it can be so tempting to place all the blame squarely on ourselves, but chances are there were some factors or people who were beyond your control. A gentle reframe could be "I contributed to the problem here, and I accept full responsibility for the part that is my fault. I understand there were factors here beyond my control. I will try to do better next time."

So there you have it: everything you need to know about reclaiming your life and reframing your story. The fundamental tenet of the Radical Reframe process is this: our lives are not determined by what happens to us but by how we interpret and react to what happens. Not by what life brings to us but by the attitude we bring to life. When we decide to be present to our lives in the moment, we give ourselves the gift of choice.

Journal: Putting it into Action

Start writing down the places where you get stuck through out the day. Carry around a little notebook with you and just jot down some key words that will trigger your memory of the struggle. At the end of the day take a look at the list and select one or two situations you would like to reframe. Write out the long version of the chosen situation, as in the exercise in Chapter 4. At the bottom of the narrative draw a line down the center of the paper, and pick out the fiction and fact components of the story. Fiction on the left, fact on the right. Bring the situation into a nonjudgmental space and ask for more information from your witness as you sift through the details and possibilities.

Slowly imagine your perspective broadening out, like a camera lens going wide, and see the situation from a broader perspective. You might even write about how significant this situation will be to you in a week, a month or a year. Write down any conclusions you made about the situation and ask yourself if this conclusion is based on fact or fiction. Then move onto some routine questions. Pick questions that resonate with you to use every time to create a new habit of thought. After a few practice runs, this way of looking at situations will become second nature. They can be questions like the following: how might other people be seeing this situation? What could I have done differently? How could I see this differently? Where is the growth in this situation? How could I put a positive spin on this situation? What would be the best-case scenario of this situation? What is this situation asking from me, what is being called to the surface of my awareness through this situation?

A good tip is to start writing down your most common negative thought patterns -- some of which you have identified in Chapter 5, and create a specific reframe for each habitual thought; potholes turn into opportunities, rascals into teachers when we actively reframe our perspective. Some of my favorite examples are: having an attitude of gratitude when doing your bills rather than allowing your mind to ruminate on lack; witnessing someone in pain becomes an opportunity to have compassion rather than hurrying by pretending not to see; recognizing grief as an invitation to honor the depths of love rather than a place to collapse into despair. Remember, you are the one writing this script, and your limiting stories are putting conditions on your life right now. So I ask you which life do you choose: one full of fear, disappointment and pain, or one full of courage, possibility and love? The choice is always ultimately yours.

Meditation: Loving Kindness

Loving Kindness meditation helps us to develop skills to deal with difficult emotional states. Many people are not taught the skills to help balance the negative pull of difficult emotions. The truth of the matter is regardless of what is going on outside of us, we can elicit feelings of love and acceptance that help to change our disposition and soften our stories. Loving Kindness Meditation is a practice that brings about positive attitudinal changes which cultivate an attitude of acceptance in our lives.

Sit in a comfortable and relaxed manner. Take a few nice slow breaths to center yourself and relax. As you breathe in, imagine drawing in fresh clean air and energy, and as you exhale imagine letting go of any thoughts or preoccupations. For a few minutes just focus on the breath moving through the center of your chest. Feel the center of your chest rise and fall. When you feel relaxed and centered begin practicing with peaceful intentions directed towards yourself. Mentally repeat, slowly and steadily, the following phrase: May I be happy, May I be safe, May I be healthy and at ease.

Focus all your attention on the intentional phrases of happiness, safety, health and ease. If your attention drifts to something else, gently redirect it back to these feelings of loving kindness. Keep repeating the phrase for a few moments, allowing yourself to feel the positive intentions you are directing towards yourself. If it makes it easier to connect with the heart energy gently place your hands over your heart. Allow yourself to connect with whatever positive feelings arise.

After a period of directing loving kindness towards yourself, bring to mind a friend or someone in your life whom you deeply love. Slowly repeat the phrases: may you be happy, may you be safe. May you be healthy and at ease. As you say the phrases in your head, feel their intention and heartfelt meaning. Imagine your friend or family member in your head as you wish them blessings from the heart. Connect with whatever positive feelings arise, as you continue to send loving kindness thoughts to a loved one.

Lastly move onto someone with whom you struggle. Bringing that person to mind and sending them your kind thoughts, repeating in your head, "May you be happy. May you be safe. May you be healthy and at ease." It may take a few practice meditation until you are able to hold someone you are struggling with in your heart and mind as you send kind thoughts. Just keep practicing. It will get easier.

Sometimes during loving kindness meditation, negative feelings may arise such as anger, grief or sadness. Take these to be signs that your heart is softening and releasing some tightly held feelings. Imagine directing loving kindness towards these thoughts. Above all, remember that there is no need to judge yourself for having your feelings. This practice is about softening our judgements and allowing the energy of loving kindness into our lives.

Reframe Wrap Up

So there you have it: the tools to change the stories that shape your life. Here is a summary of what we reviewed in this chapter. The Radical Reframe process involves perpetually changing your perspective of a situation to give it a more positive and beneficial meaning to you. The process alchemizes self-limiting beliefs and stories, to move you into a position to appreciate and accept every moment of your life. When your inner voice starts to tell a negative story or disempowering story, it is a red flag for you to pay attention and get to the work of reframing.

The first step in this process is to STOP and bring your attention back to yourself and what you are doing. Secondly, BREATHE, centering yourself by using breath mindfulness to calm your body and shake off the grip of your emotions. Try not to avoid feeling your emotions but instead to take back control from your limbic system so you can actively participate in the decision-making process of how you are going to perceive and react to a given situation. INQUIRY is the third step and offers the opportunity to tease out fact from fiction, to be able to discern the difference between the habitual stories you have been making up and the truth about what is before you, which is most often a veiled opportunity for growth and compassion. And lastly, the REFRAME determines in which direction you take all of this information. Are you going to feed the white wolf or the black wolf? Are you going to act out of fear or courage, judgement or compassion?

In every beautiful moment of your life you have the ability to write a new story -- one where you are empowered with the knowledge that you can handle anything that comes your way. The best feeling state is always available to us when we reframe the story. As you play with reframing your experiences you will learn to detect negative habits of thought and reframe them to create your own unique recipe for lasting happiness and success. With practice it will become so automatic you won't even have to think about it. Never forget, a new life story is always just a reframe away.

8

Going Deeper Within: Cultivating Self Compassion

"Your vision will become clear only when you look into your heart. Who looks outside, dreams. Who looks inside, awakens."

Carl Jung

"The curious paradox is that when I accept myself just as I am then I can change."

Carl Rogers

A Tale of Two Stories

Whitney came in to see me during a severe bout of depression, explaining how she just didn't feel happy; life seemed flat to her. I asked when was the last time she did feel happy and she could not tell me, "I feel like I have been depressed forever."

Statements such as this one signal to me a long-standing story of depression. Words like, "always" and "never" generally reflect a lack of mindfulness in our day-to-day life. We have lost touch with the waxing and waning of our moods and become over-focused on the negative. This always-or-never story line clouds our ability to acknowledge the natural ups and downs of life. It is reflective of a reliance on the limbic system to interpret what is going on in our lives because remember, the middle brain is always on the lookout for stressful, maybe even painful situations, so when we feel like all we see is bad stuff, know that it is coming from the middle brain, not conscious awareness.

Whitney went on to describe to me how hard summer time is for her because summer clothing reveals so much more of our bodies. "I just go on this hate rampage, and criticize myself repeatedly for being fat. I get so down on myself that I sabotage any attempt to diet because I figure, what is the use." Our work started, again, at ground zero: cultivating self compassion. Having worked with Whitney for 3 years I have come to know the pattern of her story. She comes to see me every August when she is feeling terribly depressed.

The past two years we worked on cultivating an awareness of the cycles of her feelings and working on her timeline. I encouraged her to start meditating, journaling and exercising. Whitney will begin a self care program and keep it up for a few months with weekly coaching sessions. When November rolls around she feels better and has forgotten the depth of her depression: in essence, she has moved on with life. Soon after, Whitney quits coming to see me. I don't usually see her again until the end of the next summer. We have gone through this three times now, and because we had access to her timeline and the diagram of her cycles, Whitney started to recognize the self-defeating pattern of her stories.

This time around, we started by reframing the intensity of her self-directed hatred with cultivating self-compassion exercises. Whitney was stuck in a self-defeating mindset, and before any true reframing could be done, she needed to work on befriending herself again. Whitney committed to restarting her daily heart meditation and walking every day. The first few sessions were very emotional as all the feelings she had been stuffing over the summer started to boil over. The major ones were the frustrations that came up each summer with her family while on their annual summer vacation and the perpetual maintenance needs of her aging home, which needed major repairs to be done during the summer weather.

It turns out that much of the negative energy she was directing at herself was actually being driven by her anger over things she felt she had no control over. Whitney hated vacationing with her family because they always fought with one another and she wanted to tell her husband she hated their house and wanted to move. But she never voiced either of these needs because she was too afraid of hurting other people's feelings. So instead she chose to take out her frustration on herself.

After one of our sessions, I started thinking about how some people become so locked in a fabricated negative story while others seem to thrive on positivity in diversity. Whitney is an average-sized woman – she certainly is not the body she describes when she talks about her negative thoughts. How could her story grow so far out of control when it is obviously not based in reality?

A great example of a radical positive reframe comes from the motivational speaker Nick Vujicic. Born in Australia to Serbian immigrants, Nick has a disabling disease called tetra-amelia, which left him with no limbs. Although he admits he suffered from depression and loneliness early in life, as he moved through his teens into adulthood he learned to reframe his disability and exploit the gifts of his situation, which was that he was *different*. He started learning to master life's daily tasks and went on to show he can do anything able-bodied people can do, from writing, typing, playing drums, to surfing.

At age 17 he began giving talks at church groups and went on to found a non-profit organization, Life Without Limbs. He has since become an international speaker, reaching out to millions of people and traveling the world. His story is amazing and inspirational, it really makes me wonder about why some people choose to disempower themselves through their negative self talk and stories rather than discover the amazing grace acquired through the reframing self acceptance and compassion.

Whitney is starting to see how she has created her own mental prison. As we returned to her timeline and she began to see the places where she is repeating a pattern of dishonesty. It became clear that her family relationships and her feelings about her home were just repeating stories of disempowerment that have popped up over the course of her life. So this is where her work began. By exploring her feelings, taking note of irritations, and starting to break them down to discover her needs. Over the next few months she made great progress in communicating with her husband her desire to have a newer, more comfortable home. After a few in-depth discussions, her husband agreed that the house was draining their resources and was taking away from time they could use to have more fun. He agreed to sell the house and start looking for something that made them both happy.

The Importance of Self Love

What Whitney lacked and Nick embraced was self-love and acceptance. Unfortunately, in our culture today, we are taught from an early age to move away from self-love and acceptance into a chronic story of self-criticism and judgement. Many of us feel a constant need to compensate for who we are with apologies, hedging words, and clarifications for our actions. We beat ourselves up for the slightest mistake and perpetually think about our flaws. We turn to other people to reflect back to us that we are okay and tell stories about being selfish when asking for what we need.

All of these examples demonstrate a lack of self love. Self love forms the foundation of your single most important relationship: with yourself. The strength of all your other relationships is exactly equal to the strength of this foundation. To love yourself is not just a self-esteem boosting piece of advice. It is the prerequisite to truly loving others. For self love is a state of appreciation for oneself that grows from beliefs and actions that support your physical, psychological and spiritual growth. Self love is dynamic and deepens as you mature. When we act in ways that support our own sense of self love, we begin to accept ourselves - with all the strengths and weaknesses - and realize we do not need defend ourselves, EVER.

Self-love is a daily practice - not a destination. To love yourself is to be in awe of the miracle of your existence. It is to deeply accept yourself - the good and the bad, the light and the dark - knowing that the real you is more than any perceived story. It is about knowing your needs, values and boundaries and honoring them above all else. Ultimately it is about being kind to yourself, treating yourself like a honored guest in your life, for you are the most important person in your life!

Take a moment to consider the things you most yearn to hear from other people. What do you daydream about other people doing for you? Whether it is that they love you, admire you, accept you for who you are, offer acts of service, physical touch or offer words of affirmation. How do you think you will feel if they were to do these things? Write down a list of all the things you desire from other people and life. Then consider, is it possible that this list reflects what you most desire from yourself? Reframe the list into positive affirmations towards yourself and start posting these throughout your home. Repeat them everyday, morning and night, and look for proof of the truth of these statements in your day to day life. As you start to incorporate these truths into your story you will find you are less needy of other people because you are giving yourself the things you need most.

The most important aspect of developing self love is remembering you are enough and you matter. We cannot know the countless number of people we touch in our lives and how we have affected them. The things we do have a ripple effect in life, as we are all intertwined, and so when we love ourselves enough to be kind, and open, and honest, we send ripples of this positive energy out into the world. Even the smallest seed of love can change another person's life.

When we gift ourselves with self-love, we cannot help but spread this story of acceptance and self celebration to others. As you give yourself permission to not be perfect, to make mistakes, and to continuously focus on the progress you are making in your life, you allow others to do the same. Love in action is the strongest force on this earth. Commit to do an act of self-love everyday. It will be a win-win for all. It provides you with an inner happiness, confidence and peace of mind that helps you to distance yourself from being swayed by outside events and opinions. It enables you to make healthier choices across all areas of your life. It frees you to celebrate in other people's strengths and good fortune rather than falling victim to the self-defeating story of "why not me." When we stop believing our stories of disempowerment, and instead choose to be fully present - right here, right now - and know we always have the power to choose ME.

To be clear, self-love is both an attitude and an act. It's how you view yourself, and how you live your life. Self-love is about tuning into your needs, honoring your body and boundaries and taking care of yourself mentally, emotionally, physically and spiritually.

The first thing you need to do to start cultivating self love is to get to know yourself. Throughout this book we have talked about utilizing mindful awareness to be present with yourself and your body. We now take this understanding a little deeper. This requires spending some time with yourself to explore your preferences. For instance, take an afternoon to go for a walk with yourself. You can go to the mall or the park or the library. As you walk, stay present with your breathing and then notice what your senses pick up. What do you smell, see, hear? How are you reacting to the things around you? What brings you pleasure on your walk? What brings you displeasure? What would you like to experience again?

Another practice is to take some time to write in your journal, answering these simple questions. What are my favorite foods? Who are my favorite people? What do I aspire to do with my life? Who do I admire? What makes me feel alive? What are the happiest parts of my life? What are my favorite memories? What parts of my life are most stressful? What brings me down? What lifts me up? What does my perfect day look like?

When cultivating self respect you must start to be mindful of who you spend your time with. Surround yourself with supportive, loving people who lift you up. Self love includes mindfully choosing the people with whom you share your life. Ask yourself, who supports me? Who do you trust? Who do you not trust? Who's really there for you? Who does things that you don't agree with? Who do you feel relaxed around? Who makes you want to be a better person?

Another component of this practice is starting to be mindful of how you talk to yourself. For many of us, self-criticism comes so naturally we don't even realize we do it. But if asked to say what goes on in our head out loud, we are able to feel the hurtful consequences of our thoughts. Each time you allow these criticisms to run rampant in your mind, you steal away your personal power. Studies have shown a direct link between self-criticism and self-esteem. On the other hand, people who score high on self-compassion are happier, better able to cope with stressors in life, and feel more content with their lives overall.

Another important factor in cultivating self-compassion is recognizing that we are all part of one huge global human community. When we see ourselves as part of a single community, we understand that everyone struggles and that we are never truly alone. This helps us to relate to others and have empathy when we see pain and know that other's will have empathy for us when we are in pain. When you catch yourself collapsing into self-judgement, ask yourself how you'd treat a friend who's experienced the same thing. What would you say? What would you not say? How would you support them? What would be the kindest way to handle to situation?

Lastly, learn to accept yourself. We all are perfectly imperfect human beings. We have our strengths and weaknesses. Accept that you are a fallible person, just like everyone else, and that you will make mistakes. In fact, you can't learn and grow if you don't identify your mistakes: so instead, revel in them. Knowing that each time you make a mistake you have an opportunity to reassess and implement a new plan of action. Accepting self means being aware of your weaknesses but also celebrating your strengths; be your best cheerleader as you stumble through this thing called life.

Ultimately self love is about recognizing you are worthy of love just because you are. Its extending compassion towards yourself and knowing you can take care of yourself no matter what happens. Self love is turning a mistake into a learning opportunity, reframing anger into acceptance and constantly reminding yourself that you are ENOUGH.

Cultivating Emotional Intimacy

I believe a large part of the crisis we have as the human "doing" is the alienation we experience from a fear of being honest about our feelings, needs and desires. We are so busy running around trying to get things done, we do not prioritize our deeper emotional needs. Quality social time has been replaced with Facebook and Twitter, and as a consequence, we have lost the security in community and family gatherings. Many people feel lonely, even when surrounded by their families, because we have lost the art of talking and listening. I refer many clients to therapy because a great deal of their angst comes from a lack of healthy and supportive relationships in their lives. We are surrounded by people all the time and yet inside we are feeling completely alienated because we are terrified of being found out as a fake and being rejected.

If we are truly seeking happiness and peace, we must be willing to be honest about who we really are. Because of our lack of trust in other people and our low feelings of self-esteem, we build relationships around false identities. We walk around hiding our true selves and then wonder why we feel lonely, less-than, or abnormal. This story of rejection of ourselves and others, prohibits us from being truly honest with our needs and desires and robs us of the gift of intimacy. Emotional intimacy is the feeling of safety and security we experience when we feel wholly accepted, respected, worthy and even admired in the eyes of our loved ones. It occurs when the communication between two people is such that it fosters the mutual sharing of their innermost selves. It is unbridled mutual self-disclosure. When we are not honest with ourselves though, we are unable to be truly honest with others and therefore feel never truly understood.

Humans are social creatures. We crave emotional closeness and thrive when we feel loved and supported and feel most alive when we are able to share our experiences and vulnerabilities with another person. But how can we share our authentic feelings, wants and needs, when we are not aware of them ourselves?

If we want to cultivate a true sense of connectedness and love, we must know and be honest about how we feel. With mindful awareness, we are able to take a step back from the hectic world, drop into how we are feeling, and then choose to allow our softer side to be revealed. We can have compassion for our fears, such as "if I voice my true opinion I may be judged" or "I'm afraid they will not like me," or "I don't feel good enough to ask for xyz."

Through out this book we have taken a good look at all the self defeating stories we tell ourselves. As we commit to creating more intimacy in our lives, as these stories arise, we can observe our fears with compassion rather than resistance. We can choose to listen to our inner fears - lean into the discomfort - rather than rejecting these fears and pushing the situation away.

Eventually we will move beyond the limiting nature of our stories into a deeper place where we can address our feelings without having to act on them. With mindful awareness we can sit quietly and allow ourselves to fully experience our emotions without retreat. After the wave of emotion has passed, we can then open ourselves to share our experiences with other people. Without the triggering nature of the limbic system, we can take care of our own emotional reactions and then turn to others for support in our processing, no longer choosing to blame or push people away. When we can take responsibility for our feelings, and have the self love it takes to care for our own needs, we can then turn to others for mutual sharing and support. The Radical Reframe process is ultimately a process of becoming a person who lives with honesty and integrity.

Stop the Insanity of Self-Judgement

One of my favorite yoga teachers encourages us to be mindful of the stories we tell ourselves during class. She'll often ask in the middle of a challenging pose, "What are you practicing right now?" Her questions usually find me completely engrossed in my own discomfort, wondering how many more minutes until class is over, all the while critically comparing my pose to the 20 year old pretzel next to me.

"Are you practicing judgment or acceptance?" she probes.

Usually this second prompt will bring me out of my diatribe and back to reality, as I ask myself, what am I practicing? Once I realize the negative cloud of judgement I am creating with my thoughts, I take a few breaths, drop back into my body and remind myself of why I come to class: I want to practice love and compassion, and yoga is a tool to strengthen this skill. So I gently laugh to myself - extending self-compassion to the part of me that is afraid or irritable or judgmental - and I come back to my mat. I then remind myself that I practice yoga to explore flexibility and strength in my mind as well as my body, so that I may carry both off my mat and into my life. I can catch myself practicing judgement and comparison again and again and again, knowing each time I can stop, center, inquire and reframe. It is a never-ending process that always brings me back to myself.

Self-judgement, which in essence is self-criticism, causes a lot of anger, anxiety and depression. It immobilizes us with a fear of making mistakes or being less than perfect and often creates a no-win situation for us as we are never happy with any results. Judging ourselves seems to be programmed into us from a very early age. We are constantly being rewarded for the right behavior, the right answer and the right attitude. In our culture being the best has the ultimate rewards, and we feel less-than if we cannot keep up. By the time we are adults, most of us have internalized a very harsh critic that seems to monitor everything we do. We have a constant running dialogue in our heads criticizing our every movement. One client explained it like this, "imagine having the critical mother monologues running 24/7. It is exhausting."

We seem to operate under the false belief that if we criticize ourselves harshly and frequently enough we will eventually get it right. Now think about that for a second. When has harsh criticism ever been helpful to you? And yet, these voices of judgement are on automatic pilot 24/7 in our heads. A young client of mine told me that every time he doesn't do well on a test, a voice inside his head says, "You're so stupid." Can you relate to this? The irony is if someone walked up to you on the street and said "You are stupid," you would probably be shocked and offended. But rarely are we shocked when we say the same thing to ourselves. Actually we say some pretty awful things to ourselves, and we think it's normal to talk to ourselves in this way: "You're fat" "you're ugly" "you're irresponsible." How many times during the day do you have a negative comment to make about yourself? I would encourage you to start monitoring these thoughts and working to reframe them. They are building the foundation for what you see in your life.

The Voices of Discontent

Where do these voices come from? Most of our self judgments are born out of stories of expectation. They are voices that have been conditioned in us, and become stories we repeatedly tell about our perceived short comings. They may have come from our family, friends, neighbors or teachers at school. They come from the media in the form of messages on beauty, success and thinness. These messages are painfully unrealistic. Yet the story of having these equating to success and happiness are so strong we strive to obtain that which we know is unattainable and beat ourselves up with self judgement when we do not achieve these standards. In the end, we can never be perfect. We can only learn to reframe our experience to know that we are perfectly imperfect and doing the best that we can. We can learn to find the blessings of love and joy in every experience along the way.

It is important to differentiate between *negative judgement* and *discernment*. Discernment is the ability to judge well a situation and involves going deeper than the mere acceptance of a perception into the true meaning of a situation. Discernment is the *integration of inquiry and reframing*. A discerning individual is considered to possess wisdom, and be of sound judgement that can result in growth and healing. Discernment as applied to reframing means the ability to recognize where you are starting to fall into your story. It involves identifying when you need to pull back and center and then separate out fact verses fiction. For instance, if you lose your job, then you lost your job. That does not mean you are stupid, a failure, or destined to never succeed. These are judgements: very negative, self-defeating judgements. The reframe might be that there is a better job out there for you, that your former job was not a good fit. Perhaps you are in the wrong career and your best life path would be to go back to school, stay home with your children, or take care of an ailing family member.

Judgment, on the other hand, is imbued with aversion, a desire for something to be different. Judgement comes into action when we are making comparisons, judging what is supposed to be happening or what would be preferable. When we judge, we assume we know the answer, and generally we do not. Especially when it involves other people. Because we are so alienated from our needs we often do not know what is best for ourselves, and we cannot possibly know what is best for someone else.

Through mindfulness practice and self-inquiry, you can begin to neutralize the power of self-judgement and reframe your criticisms in a different light. By softening your inner critic, you free yourself to just *be*. It takes time to sift out the self judgement and learn to release criticism to transform your stories to support a sense of well-being and openness to new possibilities. Hidden gold will appear when you let go of your negative-judgments. With mindful curiosity you will be able to see under the judgement aspects of yourself that you never saw before; discovering new strengths and perspectives will carry you towards a new and better story of your life.

Letting Go of Resistance

Have you ever had that experience of being so engrossed in an activity that you lose track of time? We all have this ability to suspend awareness of ourselves and our surroundings, when we allow ourselves to get caught up in the energy of joy overlapping with deep concentration. This is the flow. Most people love it because while in the flow, we drop all expectations and just allow ourselves to be a focused stream of consciousness.

Getting into the flow of your life means letting go of resistance. Often I see clients resisting what is and causing themselves great pain and suffering in the process. At any moment, your situation is the way it is whether you like it or not. When you fight the truth of the way your situation is, you create a state of fear, upset, and tunnel vision. We waste so much time clinging to an inner state of resistance. Letting go and getting into the flow means you are committed to letting go of resistance and committed to seeing life as it is happening, and not just how you want it to be. This is why meditation is so helpful for our well-being. It invites us to get out of our stories, with all their judgements and expectations, and allows us to enter the flow of life.

I was recently paddle-boarding with friends and having a hard time enjoying the adventure. I was hot, the water was rough, and I had forgotten to put sunscreen on my feet, of all things. My mind was going crazy with all that was wrong until I caught myself, stopped, centered, and reframed the situation. I took a few breaths, smiled to myself, and then started focusing on what a beautiful day it was, how lucky I was to be out on the water with people I loved and getting an occasional heart leaping glimpse of dolphins swimming nearby. Within minutes of my actively switching my thoughts, I became aware that I was animatedly chatting about my book and laughing with my friends. It just took a little awareness of my stinking thinking to be able to let go, get into the flow, and experience the delicious shift in my mood in a matter of minutes as I reframed the focus of my thoughts. And in the end, my feet did not get sunburned: it had been wasted thought energy.

Letting go is the inner action that allows us to flow with whatever life presents. The moment you let go of your expectations, you allow yourself the freedom to flow with life and restore your ability to see clearly. You are able to access your inner creativity and see solutions that were not possible within the realm of your narrow expectations. Solutions you could never have seen before.

Much of our fear is created out of the resistance to flow with life. For example, if you have a fear of losing someone, you are resisting the future story called, "losing a person I love." The more time you spend thinking about your fear of losing the person, the bigger your fear becomes. The bigger your fear, the more threatened you feel. The more threatened you feel, the more you are preoccupied with the looming event and less able to be present with that person now. By resisting the future event, you cheat yourself out of the experience of having them in your life right now!

Opening Your Heart to Vulnerability

As I pointed out earlier in this chapter, many of us are walking around afraid to let people know who we truly are. We hide our true feelings and selves in many ways. Coffee masks our fatigue like alcohol masks our feelings, humor can mask our anger, and false smiles mask our fear. We hide behind clothes, cars and homes. We identify ourselves by our education, job or social status. We hide because we fear we will be hurt or rejected if we let our true selves be known. We are terrified of feeling vulnerable to attack, as if anyone could take away who or what we are with their thoughts. But this is the reality: we hide because we are afraid of what other people think. And because of this fact, we are allowing ourselves to be controlled by someone else's thoughts.

Remember: the only thing we can control is ourselves. We can monitor our thoughts and the reactions they solicit in our bodies and minds, and we can control our behaviors and actively choose to act with integrity, honesty and sincerity regardless of the circumstances. We all need to be seen authentically for who we are. It's part of what makes us human. Just watch a child flourish under the attention of a group of adults. The joy they feel by being seen is contagious. When we don't allow ourselves to be seen, we diminish our importance in this world. We under-value ourselves. We deprive ourselves of the opportunity to contribute to the evolution of the things that bring us meaning: our friends and families, our communities, as well as the evolution of consciousness on this planet.

A life of joy is one in which we feel comfortable letting our true selves shine in the world. It means accepting the fact that we're going to stumble over our words sometimes, be misunderstood, and even, at times, disliked. We are going to make mistakes - sometimes big ones - and we will be okay. We all make mistakes. This process is opening up to being vulnerable. Vulnerability is allowing ourselves to be open to being wounded or attacked. It is a willingness to trust that you will be okay, an attitude that basically says "here I am world, say what you will, but I know I am good and doing my best." Vulnerability means we embrace intimacy in our lives knowing that we risk being hurt. It is the tilling of the soil for seeds of happiness and joy.

Our job is to face the fear of being wounded or hurt, and stand there in all of its discomfort. When you can meet your own vulnerability without pushing against it, the richness of life opens up to you. All the higher emotions - generosity, gratitude, compassion, forgiveness, and especially, humility - emerge from this place of openness and acceptance. To recognize your vulnerability is to connect up with both the mystery of life and the mystery of how life can be so wondrous and beautiful, yet simultaneously so absolutely terrible.

The beauty is, once you harness your fear and embrace your vulnerability, you begin to see there is a part of you that truly is invulnerable. We all possess an inner light, drive, knowledge, call it what you will, but it is what makes each of us uniquely beautiful. If you have done the exercises in this book and cultivated a meditative practice and a safe space, you will realize the world can never take that away from you. Through these practices you may begin to understand that we each have a choice as to how we feel and how we act in the world.

This is the power of vulnerability. When we drop all the pretenses and masks, allow ourselves to flow with life and be open to what life serves up, we can choose to move towards happiness, love, and peace. Vulnerability breaks us open to the truth of our hearts, which is love. We all are beings of love, and nothing can destroy that.

Journal: A Love Letter to Yourself

I firmly believe in order for us to change the world, we must start with ourselves. Self-love offers us the opportunity to see we are all perfectly imperfect. It is the human condition to be imperfect: understanding and accepting our inadequacies enriches the experience of being human. How would we be able to have compassion for others' struggles if we did not understand our own? I would like for you to consider the things you least like about yourself, bringing to mind your biggest inadequacies. Consider the things that bring on feelings of shame, insecurity and vulnerability. What feelings come up when you consider this aspect of yourself? Write these feelings down.

Now write a letter to yourself in your journal from the perspective of a friend or family member who loves you unconditionally. This exercise mirrors the heart meditation we did at the beginning of this book, so remember if you cannot think of anyone, bring to mind a guardian angel or your higher self. Imagine this person can see all of your strengths and weaknesses, including the aspects you are writing about in this journal entry. Reflect upon how this person or entity loves you unconditionally, write about how you are loved and accepted by them exactly as you are. In his/her great wisdom, this person knows all you have been through in life and understands why you behave the way your do. They understand all of the millions of things that have happened to you up to this point to make you the person that you are today, and they love you for your courage, strength, and resilience. This individual sees all that you are capable of and knows you are doing your best right now. Include variations of this in your letter.

What things would this being say to you to ease your suffering and self-judgement? What changes might they suggest for the future, not because they judge you, but because they only want the best possible future for you and your loved ones? As you write from the perspective of this benevolent being, try to infuse the letter with a strong sense of acceptance, kindness, and encouragement for your utmost happiness and success in life. Remember to sign the letter: Love, Me.

Return to this letter as often as you like, using it as a type of pep talk or reality check to remind you of the truth of who you are. Love, connection and acceptance are your birthright, and the only way to claim them is to make them a part of your story.

Meditation: Cultivating Gratitude

Gratitude means thankfulness, counting your blessings, noticing simple pleasures, and acknowledging the abundant nature of all you receive in your life. It means learning to live your life as if everything were a miracle, and being aware on a continuous basis of how much you've been given. Gratitude shifts your focus from what your life lacks to the abundance that is already present. In addition, behavioral and psychological research has shown the surprising life improvements that can stem from the practice of gratitude. Giving thanks makes people happier and more resilient, it strengthens relationships, it improves health, and it reduces stress. This gratitude meditation will help you to cultivate more gratitude in your life. It will help you realize the power of the two most important words in our lives: THANK YOU.

Find a comfortable sitting position, where you can feel your feet planted firmly on the earth, and your spine feels supported by the back of a chair or cushion. Take a few moments to connect with your breath, breathing in and out, allowing yourself to let go of any thoughts and bring your full focus onto your breath. Once you start to feel relaxed start cultivating gratitude for your body, and for the ability to breathe. While focusing on being grateful for the freedom your body gives you, allow the feeling to naturally arise in your heart space. Acknowledge your beating heart, breathing lungs and all the cells in your body that are functioning around the clock so you may exist.

Give thanks for your physical body, feeling gratitude for the ability to move and function in this world. Feel gratitude for the ability you have to communicate. Acknowledge your strengths and weaknesses, being grateful for the opportunity to move through life, to grow and expand, and to love.

Take a moment to bring your awareness to your feet and feel how they physically connect with the earth. Acknowledge that the earth below your feet nurtures all life on this planet. Feel grateful for the support and nourishment you receive from the earth, and feel grateful for all the life that the earth supports - from your family, to your community, to your country, to all sentient beings.

Move your thoughts to the abundance of life found in nature. Send out a peaceful "thank you" to the animal kingdom and all the beautiful wonders you have witnessed in the natural world. Bringing to mind the forests, oceans, lakes, deserts. Imagine the trees and flowers and plants.

Allow yourself to sense a deep gratefulness for the inter-dependence of all life, where everything has a role and purpose. Be thankful for the wisdom to be able to appreciate this connection.

Now move your gratitude to all of the people in your life and the roles they play to help you grow in love. Feel thankful for your family and friends, coworkers and neighbors. Imagine the timeless lineage of your ancestry, feel grateful for all of your ancestors that came before you, and paved the way for you to come into existence.

Extend gratitude out to all the people that you don't know but who make your life possible: the farmers, the truck drivers, the people who made the clothes you wear. The teachers who taught you in school and the health care providers who have helped you when you were sick. Send out a heart felt thanks to each of those people and any others that may come to mind. Then switch to all the people you touch in your life with your work. Feel gratitude for the opportunity to serve.

Now move into the specific things in your life for which you are grateful. It might be your home, your job, music, art, your garden. Whatever brings you joy, bring that into your awareness right now and feel the gratitude you have for these things enhancing your life. Bringing beauty and love to your heart.

Feel gratitude for free will, and the ability you possess to create whatever life experience you want to live. Expand that gratitude out to encompass all the darkness, fear and pain in the world. For it is in these situations that we have the opportunity to rise to our greatest heights. For it is this darkness in the human psyche that creates through pain, the shattering moments of joy and love that enrich our journey through life. Feel grateful for it all.

The Gift of Self Compassion

There is a simple Buddhist definition of compassion that goes like this: "When love meets suffering and stays loving, that's compassion." Compassion is a deep feeling for a suffering individual with the wish and effort to alleviate it. Self-compassion is this desire directed towards oneself. It means treating ourselves with the same kindness and understanding with which we'd want to treat someone we truly love. Self-compassion is extending compassion to one's self in instances of perceived inadequacy, failure, or general suffering. When we are able to be gentle with ourselves - extending a hand of kindness and warmth rather than judgement and criticism - we teach ourselves the world is actually a very safe place. We are then able to share this trusting belief with other people through our conscious actions of compassion.

The fear of facing our own pain is so strong, and the story our culture has taught us to avoid our feeling and hide our authentic selves is so strong, that many of us are just moving through our lives on automatic pilot. When we stop to take some time to get to know our own heart, observing our actions and behaviors and inquiring as to why we are where we are in our lives, we gift ourselves with the ability to change our story.

As Carl Rogers famously wrote, "The curious paradox is that when I accept myself just as I am, then I can change." When we surrender our resistance, and let go of all the ways we hide ourselves, we are able to see the totality of our humanity. This surrender offers an opportunity to accept it in full, the struggle, the uncertainty, the vulnerability, and the confusion we experience in life. This is the greatest gift we can give ourselves, the gift of true, whole-hearted compassion for this experience called life. The best we can hope for is to have the awareness of how we affect our lives and the world, the courage to stand in our own imperfection and know we are enough, and to embrace with self compassion our transgressions, knowing that there will always be a next time to get it right. The entire process of reframing our lives is to let go of who we think we were supposed to be and embrace who we truly are. So go out there and thrive in all your imperfect beauty.

Epilogue

$\mathcal{E}$ach year, I gather with my women's group to do a New Years' meditation to determine an intention for the upcoming year. I will guide the group through a visualization of reviewing the past year and then imagine standing on the precipice of the new year and ask the group to consider what they want to create. It has become the apex of our group gatherings and everyone looks forward to discovering what their *word* for the upcoming year will be.

This year I changed the meditation a bit and opened it up to planting multiple seeds of intention, rather than just coming up with one word. After I had recorded the meditation and did it myself, I was floored at the insight I gained by reviewing my year. This practice has become such an invaluable tool to see how I have progressed through out the year, what stories I am still telling that limit my potential, but also what successes I had that moved me closer to my goals and deepened my awareness of self.

On January 20th, 2017, I was sitting on a train, headed to Washington DC with two of my closest friends, Kelly and Karla, and a friend Kelly had invited, Char, who flew in from Chicago the day before. We were going to participate in the Women's March on Washington. As we had a 4 hour train ride, Kelly thought it would be a good time to do the meditation and talk about our expectations of the upcoming year. We each did the meditation and then starting discussing the insights we gained afterwards.

This year was a year of perceived loss for me. After my divorce 4 years prior, I had intentionally reached out to my friends at work for support and surrounded myself with a core group of women who were so inspiring and uplifting, that my relationship with them has changed my life. It was the first time I ever allowed myself to be truly vulnerable and open to a group of women. In many ways, they became my soul sisters.

Over the course of the past year, though, they all had made the difficult decision to leave our practice and create their own practices together. I was devastated. I literally cried for months, feeling a profoundly deep pain of abandonment. I was unable to go with them because of the perimeters of my profession, as a physician assistant I am required to work with a doctor who agrees to supervise me, and therefore am unable to practice on my own. And so my wounded brain kept replaying a very familiar story of *abandonment* and always *feeling left out.* Just thinking of them working side by side, seeing each other every day, laughing and processing, would put me in a tail spin, even after they all told me it was not like that. They hardly saw one another. But the wounded pull was so strong I could not convince my mind that the story I was telling was untrue.

With the support of my soul sisters, and my new therapist, whom I sought out after three months of misery, I processed through my grief and fear, and slowly began to reframe the story. My wise friend Kelly pointed out on the train that a few weeks ago she noticed I had shifted my story from "when you guys abandoned me" to "when you guys left." Her insight along with the insight I gained from the meditation made me see that I had healed both of those very old, painful stories: I am always abandoned by the ones I love and I do not belong anywhere.

By leaning into my grief and pain, allowing my friends to witness my struggle and support me, I was able to heal a very deep wound of abandonment stemming from my biological father abandoning me and my mother when I was 1 year old. By being able to hold a space for myself, stay centered in my feelings, and look for meaning outside of the old story of being abandoned and feeling left out, I had healed my worst fear. I now know, I can never be abandoned.

The story I had held so close to my heart about not being valuable enough for someone to stay was only being perpetuated because I was abandoning myself by not trusting my choices and my feelings. With the help of my closest friends, I could see that even though the circumstances of our external relationship had changed, we had not changed; they still loved me, and I them. In fact, now their friendship is even more valuable to me because we all have to make a concerted effort to stay in one another's lives. This is something I took for granted when they each were just down the hall.

And so, on the train, as we were processing our experience in the meditation, I explained my insight and also the satisfaction I gained from knowing that I had learned to trust my own heart and befriend myself. I said, "I am so proud of myself because through this very difficult year, I have learned that I am lovable and that I am valuable as a friend." And yet after I said it, the old story of being unlovable reared its head. Honoring my insecurity, I turned to my friend Karla and asked a very vulnerable question, "I am a good friend, aren't I?" And she smiled back at me with warmth in her eyes and said "yes Lara you are."

～ ～

When we are able to know our hearts and minds, and share our experiences with others, amazing things can happen. We begin to realize that we are not at all alone, that we are just having a human experience, with all its beautiful ups and downs. When we allow people into our lives, and into our hearts, we begin to understand that we are all in this together.

When we can all expose our under bellies - the parts of us that we hide out of shame or distrust - we realize in the end we all just want to feel accepted, safe and loved. But really this acceptance, safety and love is a gift we give ourselves. And once you have this truth, your heart will soften to all beings, knowing there is nothing to prove, nothing to do but share in love.

That is what the Radical Reframe process is all about: helping people to let go of the stories that keep them separate, alone and in pain. It is a process of opening up to the truth of who you are: a human being having a human experience. If you are living in pain, it is a world you subtly and unintentionally created out of your own chosen stories and beliefs.

Remember, freedom from chronic suffering is just a reframe away. This is what the world needs now more than ever: each one of us working on our own process towards truth and love and vulnerability. When we find it, it will radiate out from our hearts and heal the world.

As we learn through reframing to turn towards what feels good: peace, kindness, love, compassion, acceptance, OUR HEARTS WILL BE RE-AWAKENED and HEALED. As we heal the wounds of our past, lighten our burdens, and open our hearts up to vulnerability, we will give others permission to do the same. This is the ultimate reframe, a reframing of the collective consciousness of fear, distrust and pain into an awakening to the truth of all that it means to be human - to experience love, joy and connectedness. If we choose to reframe our current path, this can be our destiny. We have the power to forever change the world for the good if we start living our lives based on self-awareness and the quest to improve the stories we tell every step of the way. I believe the words of Lao Tzu summarize the Radical Reframe process beautifully, and so I will conclude with the following:

Watch Your thoughts
For they become words
Watch your words
For they become actions
Watch your actions
For they become character
Watch your character
It becomes your destiny

Acknowledgements

This book would never have made it without the support of my aunt, Rhonda Hughes, and the rest of my family: my mother, Marsha Hoiberg, my sister, Jill Kain and my father, John Kain. I'd like to thank my brother, Mark Kain, for encouraging me to reframe my expectations and embrace an alternative career path which made this book possible. Thank you to the most amazing group of women I consider my soul sisters: Erin McCord, Karla Drake and Kelly Scharver. Your willingness to be open, honest and vulnerable with me has catapulted me into healing so much distortion within my heart. As co-creators of The Tapestry Book club, I am grateful to be walking beside each of you on our path of self-awareness and enlightenment. To Nicole Sanderlin, Ehsaneh Sadr, Marc Stachurski, Amy Riek, Robert Bruce, Chris Younkins and Kathy Brasington: thank you for always providing a listening ear, believing I would finish this project and that it might actually be good. A huge shout out to my proof readers, Char Bennington, Gary Youngblood and Grace Tazewell. Your willingness to help me sift through pages and pages of words to find just the right ones is truly *priceless*. To my wonderfully supportive and wickedly talented editor, Wendy Levinson, for her enduring support, positive pep talks and insightful edits to my manuscript. And lastly, I acknowledge my constant companions, Harry and Dupree, the four-legged beings of unconditional love that feel it is their job to perpetually pull me out of angst and anxiety into remembering that life is just one big joyful ride. My heart spills over with gratitude for all of the abundance in my life! I am truly blessed!

Made in the USA
Middletown, DE
08 January 2020